Get Your

$\dfrac{\text{Act}}{\text{Together}}$

D0361926

OTHER BOOKS BY PAM YOUNG AND PEGGY JONES

Sidetracked Home Executives

The Sidetracked Sisters Catch-up on the Kitchen

The Sidetracked Sisters' Happiness File

Get Your Act Together

A 7-Day Get-Organized Program for the Overworked, Overbooked, and Overwhelmed

Pam Young and Peggy Jones, D.E.*

HarperPerennial
A Division of HarperCollins Publishers

*Deficiency Experts

Material on pp. 41-42 reprinted from the *Money Extra* issue of *Money* Magazine by special permission; copyright 1990, Time, Inc.

GET YOUR ACT TOGETHER. Copyright © 1993 by Pam Young and Peggy Jones. All rights reserved. Printed in the United States of America. No part of this book may be used or reproduced in any manner whatsoever without written permission except in the case of brief quotations embodied in critical articles and reviews. For information address HarperCollins Publishers, Inc., 10 East 53rd Street, New York, NY 10022.

HarperCollins books may be purchased for educational, business, or sales promotional use. For information, please write: Special Markets Department, HarperCollins Publishers, Inc., 10 East 53rd Street, New York, NY 10022.

FIRST EDITION

Designed by George J. McKeon

Library of Congress Cataloging-in-Publication Data

Young, Pam (Pamela I.)
    Get your act together. : a 7-day get-organized program for the overworked, overbooked, and overwhelmed / Pam Young and Peggy Jones. — 1st ed.
        p. cm.
    ISBN 0-06-096991-1 (pbk.)
    1. Home economics. 2. Housewives—Time management. I. Jones, Peggy (Peggy A.) II. Title.
TX147.Y67 1993
640—dc20   93-17065

93 94 95 96 97 ❖/RRD 10 9 8 7 6 5 4 3

We dedicate this book to the American family.

The history of humanity is not the history of its wars, but the history of its households.
— JOHN RUSKIN, 1819–1900

Contents

Acknowledgments

We want to thank the two men in our lives, Danny and Terry, but there aren't words meaningful enough (not even in the synonym finder) to express the depth of our gratitude.

We want to give special thanks to each of our children: Michael, Peggy, Joanna, Chris, Jeff, and Allyson, for being guinea pigs for all of our bright ideas.

At the risk of sounding like an Academy Awards acceptance speech, we must thank our parents for raising us to believe that success comes from having a positive attitude even in negative circumstances. Growing up, we were allowed to be discouraged, depressed, angry, or in a bad mood, but Mom was always there with a timer and we had ten minutes to get through it and get on with life. The timer has come in handy during the evolvement of our new system.

Special thanks to John Boswell for his friendship over the last fifteen years. It is a privilege to be part of his flock of authors. His enthusiasm, wonderful sense of humor, and his kindness to strangers has always been an attraction to us.

Our wonderful friend, Kac Young, deserves special thanks for her daily, long-distance hotline of quality feedback. She has been a great cheerleader for this book, but, just as valuable, she has had the courage to tell us when something didn't work. We have always respected her professional advice, but her personal friendship is priceless.

Thanks go to Sydney Craft Rozen, for once again saving us from literary embarrassment. To have Sydney help us over the last fifteen years has been a real blessing. Her unique ability to edit a manuscript, without changing the voice of the author, is rare and truly appreciated.

Nancy Peske, our editor at HarperCollins, deserves special acknowledgment. She can giggle and edit brilliantly at the same time. It was great working with her.

One

What Is a Person Like You Doing in a Mess Like This?

We know what kind of a mess you are in right now. We could tell you, in detail, what your kitchen, living room, closets, cupboards, drawers, car, purse, refrigerator, and even your bedroom look like. No, we're not psychic, and no, we haven't been sneaking around your house, peeking in your windows at night. We know because we used to be in the same messy dilemma. We escaped and have helped thousands of other people get free from the vicious grip of disorganization. We can help you do it, too.

You know you are overworked, overbooked, and overwhelmed, but did you know that maybe one of the main reasons you got that way is because you were born that way? We believe that if you have struggled to be organized but still lead a messy and disorganized life, you can blame it on heredity. It's our guess that your mess is genetic, and if we're right about that, we can tell a lot more about you.

Instead of reading this book, you're probably supposed to be doing something else. Maybe you're in a bookstore at the mall when you should be picking up vacuum cleaner bags at Sears. Or maybe you're propped up on your bed reading and you should be starting dinner. One woman in a small midwestern town wrote and said that she "accidentally" ran into one of our books. She had locked herself out of her house in bare feet and no coat. It was the dead of winter and her first thought was the "warm" library that was just a block from her home. Once inside, she called her husband to bring her a key and made a decision to get organized. The librarian, able to size up the reader, led the trembling, shoeless woman to our book.

We bet you've tried to get organized in the past. In fact, you've probably gone off on organizational binges with great energy and enthusiasm, only to end up with one more discarded clutterbuster to add to your stash of gadgets and papers. We suspect that you have a lot of organizational tools around the house: filing cabinets, shoe trees, stacking bins, pen caddies, and mail organizers. But instead of satisfying your organizational needs, these tools just loom like lighthouses in a sea of clutter and chaos, beaming rays of accusation that you didn't follow through.

Maybe you also have a diary, photo albums, weekly planners, and calendars that are blank or only partially filled out. Perhaps you bought a rowing machine, stationary bicycle, NordicTrack, Thigh Master, or Gut Buster, but you're not rowing, biking, tracking, squeezing, or busting. In fact, your exercise has probably been limited to hauling all that equipment from the attic to the driveway for a garage sale every couple of years.

Speaking of exercise, do you belong to a health club that you don't go to? Speaking of health, did you invest in the Richard Simmons Deal-a-Meal cards, but the last time you dealt them, you left them in your bathrobe and they went through the wash? Is your *Meet You at the Top* motivational tape at the bottom of the bill basket? Did you buy

Pull Your Own Strings but still find yourself at the end of your rope?

Have you ever been a victim of PREMATURE EVALUATION? Any time you've tried to get organized but had to look for a pen, unload a chair, and clear a spot on the kitchen table for a piece of scratch paper, you've jumped the organizational gun. In the end, you have suffered the letdown and disappointment of premature evaluation. Embarrassed at ending up in more of a mess than you had when you started, you're left with battered self-esteem and public failure (usually logged by family and friends.)

The reason we know so much about you is that we are deficiency experts. We really do think that being disorganized is genetic. As you will read in Chapter 2, we inherited our messy genes from our dad. For more than fifteen years, we have made it our mission to help people who were born with the congenital tendency to be locked out, left behind, and overdrawn.

We think people who are prompt and efficient are born that way, too. They're those few naturally organized people who have it together. They have five- and ten-year plans; they floss, make lists, and actually do the stuff on the lists. They don't run anywhere, look for anything, arrive late, or forget birthdays. They have low cholesterol, IRAs, cash in their wallets, milk in the refrigerator, and high-fiber cereal in the cupboard ... and they were all born on their due dates! They're people like Ordell Daily, our make-believe Goddess of Order, who has a standing hair appointment on Saturday, sleeps on her face Saturday night, and comes to church Sunday morning, resprayed with Follicle Freeze and looking brittle yet lifelike.

> *Ordell Daily was an organized soul.*
> *No one could match her skill.*
> *The crack of dawn was her rising time,*
> *Her day was a routine drill.*

Showered and dressed in less than ten,
Breakfast in just under three.
Dishes cleared, the dusting done,
She knew she wouldn't be free

'til the table was set for dinner
And the bathrooms were sanitized,
And the plants in her terrarium
Were properly fertilized,

And the pile of ironing nagging her,
Just a blouse and her husband's shirt,
Were pressed to their perfection
And put away so they wouldn't hurt
The streamlined look in her laundry room,
A sight not seen by most;
With its white and shiny counters
And appliances she could boast
Were cleaned on the inside,
Polished on the out
Twice a day with the right amount
Of elbow grease and Lemon Pledge.
She'd even polish the window ledge,

Then back upstairs to make the bed,
Brush her teeth while her prayers were said.
Vacuum carpets, check the clock,
Exactly time to wake the flock.
"Get up, kids, it's time to rise."
Back downstairs to bake some pies.

At eight when the kids got on the bus,
Her day had just begun.
She didn't waste a moment,
But worked straight through to one.

At one she ate an apple
While she wrote a menu plan,
Answered several letters
Then off to the store she ran.

She never had to look for things
They were always in their place.
Her hair was always perfect,
She had makeup on her face.

She never missed appointments,
And she'd always get there early.
Tardy wasn't ever part
Of her vocabulary.

That's why it's so ironic
That when her name was in the news,
A synonym for tardy
Was the word the writer used.

The column in the paper said,
"Ordell was thirty-four."
She left behind a tidy home
From the ceiling to the floor.

Ordell never played in life,
She worked to her demise.
The writer named the funeral home
Where the "LATE" Ordell Daily lies.

Do you know somebody like Ordell? If you do, you've probably envied her ability to get so much accomplished, and you've wondered how she does it. God made one Ordell to every ten people like you. That's because Ordell does the work of ten people, and she needs people like you to create work for her. You see, it all goes back to genetics. Ordell doesn't have a creative organ in her body. Her gift is an operative left brain.

Undoubtedly you have heard or read about studies of the right and left brain. If you look at a diagram of the human brain, you'll see that it is divided in half. One half takes care of creative information such as music, color, imagination, and intuition. That's the right side, and people who are predominantly right-brained are artists, musicians, actors, writers, etc. The other half of the brain keeps track of numbers, time, direction, logic, and practical information. That's the left side; people who are predominantly left-brained are scientists, mathematicians, computer wizards, bookkeepers, and people like Ordell. *You* were born with a left brain that isn't hooked up and a right brain that is overactive and renders you organizationally impaired.

Here's what happens. You start out on a project, and with the help of your well-developed right brain you dive in with great imagination and enthusiasm. It doesn't matter what the project is; it can be something as simple as changing the oil in the car or washing the breakfast dishes, or as complex as making a dress or building a carport. The important thing to note is that, at some point, you'll hit the boring part of the project. (Every project has one.) When you come to that cheerless place, your right brain will always kick in with an alternative list of activities. It works like the remote control to the television in the hands of a husband. You just get interested in a project and, BANG, a new program. Depending on how much energy you have, you can start so many things that you could end up talking to the fruit in your wallpaper.

If you were to try to be like Ordell, you would not be happy. You would overgoal yourself into a frenzy and end up mean and cranky. We think books like *The Seven Habits of Highly Effective People,* by Stephen Covey, were written for people like Ordell, who are already highly effective. We made up our own seven habits, which are more realistic for people like us.

Seven Habits of Minimally Effective People

1. Plan your appointments around the *TV Guide.*
2. Every fourth day, stay in your pajamas and be a zero.
3. When you get the mail, allow at least thirty minutes to focus your complete attention on filling out all the Publisher's Clearing House stuff.
4. Aim low so you won't be disappointed.
5. Go to bed at nine and get up at nine.
6. Surround yourself with pets, children, and friends.
7. Dress for comfort. Before adding an item to your wardrobe, ask yourself, "Could I sleep in this?"

Once you get realistic about what you are doing with your life, you can begin to take steps to improve it and still enjoy the easygoing kind of person you are and always will be. It's also very important to keep in mind that getting organized is really as simple as breathing. You are going to discover that it is NOT the mountain you think it is.

Five Steps Out of Your Messy Dilemma

Step One: Awareness
The first step out of clutter and chaos into peace, joy, success, and order in your life is to become aware of how your organizationally impaired mind works. Being organized really is a matter of MIND management, not time management. We have experimented with our own minds and have been able to pinpoint the exact time into a pro-

ject that the right brain gets a new idea. This depends, in part, on how interesting the activity is and at what point it becomes boring. You can try this experiment with your own brain:

At the end of this paragraph, put the book down and find a boring project. It could be a load of clothes to fold or a bed to make. You could shave or peel potatoes, or, if you can find a pen and paper, you could start writing the alphabet over and over. What you need to do is see just how far into the project you go before IT happens. If you don't want to do this experiment now, remember it the next time you are faced with a boring task, which won't be long, because life is full of boring projects. It's our guess that you'll get about six seconds into the job when a conniving little thought will subtly sneak its way in and say, "MMM, there's leftover pie in the refrigerator," or "Hey, shouldn't you see if there's any mail?" or "Oh, let's call Mom and see how she is."

Once you are aware that this is what happens and that it's behind all of your unfinished business, you can be prepared for the interruption. A split second after the launch of the thought, you'll be able to intercept it before it can destruct your work.

People with our problem have reported as many as a dozen of these mental interruptions in a single minute! You will be able to significantly stifle this sidetracking trigger in your brain if you get in the habit of recognizing it. Then all you have to do is stand up to it and stop it immediately. Think of the sound of an air horn at a basketball game and, if you have to, simulate its sound with your own voice. Whenever you start to wander, give yourself a blast on your air horn. (Don't worry if people look at you as if you are weird. Just smile and say, "I hate it when that happens.")

One young mother told us that the "air horn" had made her very aware of what her right brain was doing to sidetrack her. She said that now that she is aware, at least she has a choice to stay on track or be distracted. Before, she just unconsciously ended up somewhere else in the house, doing something else. Now she is able to accomplish so much more than before.

Step Two: Appreciate Yourself

The second step is to appreciate your own positive qualities. Think about yourself for a minute. You own some of the most valuable qualities a person can have. You are spontaneous, creative, flexible, optimistic, and friendly. Yet with all of these wonderful qualities, how is it that you are in the mess you are in? The reason is that every virtue has a fault at the other end. In fact, a fault IS a virtue ... left unchecked.

Take your OPTIMISM, for example. You have a positive outlook and great intentions. You might put a pile of stuff on the stairs, convinced that you'll take it up on your next trip. But the next trip doesn't include the waiting pile; instead, you start a new pile at the top of the stairs, planning to take it on the next trip down. You keep adding to the piles with the best of intentions, and, before you know it, you'd be risking suicide to maneuver the stairs with even a small armload. The only way down is the banister.

FLEXIBILITY is another of your great assets. You could go down the banister just as easily as take the conventional way. You are able to conform to many molds (even when they're growing on the food in the refrigerator). You are like a good set of shocks. Your easygoing nature can cope quite nicely with all the little bumps and holes in the road of life. But the trouble is, if the road doesn't get fixed, the bumps get bigger, the holes get deeper, and the road to life turns into a pathway to CHAOS (the "Can't Have Anyone Over Syndrome").

When you can't have anyone over, you aren't happy,

because another of your qualities is FRIENDLINESS. Because you are friendly, you are popular and almost everybody loves you. Consequently, you are on the phone so much that your listening ear is flatter than the one out in the open. If you go to the store and run into one of your many friends, you can totally lose track of time and the reason you are even at the store. People love to be around you because you are playful and fun-loving. You love to laugh, dance, sing, and play with kids and animals, and you welcome interruptions from boring or routine work.

You are SPONTANEOUS. You can switch direction like an expert skateboarder. That's because you rarely have a direction. Interruptions are a signal to move on to something more interesting. You aren't ruffled by a change in plans, because your plans are usually roaming around in your right brain. Because of your hyperactive right brain, you are very creative.

CREATIVITY is a priceless commodity. It builds bridges, scripts movies, and writes love songs and best-selling novels. Creativity sets fashion trends and paints priceless works of art. Unfortunately, creativity costs a lot of money if you're disorganized. We think we know why Picasso had to charge so much for his paintings. It's probably because he needed to recoup all the money he'd spent on craft supplies before he got organized. Like Picasso, we too have gone nuts in a craft store. Once we spent over $150 on silk flowers, faux gems, ribbon, fabric paint, and beads at the Ric Rac Craft Shack, and all we'd gone there to buy was a new glue gun and some styrofoam balls.

We have often been introduced as the Slob Sisters, which has always been okay with us, except that we get quite a few letters from people who say that the word "slob" is too harsh and that it conjures up a vision of a dirty, smelly person who spends most of the time propped in front of a TV set, slugging down pork rinds and guzzling cases of generic beer. We therefore decided to make each letter in the word "slob" stand for a quality that most disorganized people possess.

> S stands for spontaneous.
> L stands for lighthearted.
> O stands for optimistic.
> B stands for beloved.

Now that you see that the main reason you are in a mess is because you are such a fine person, it's time to move on to step three.

STEP THREE: FIND A REASON

The third step is to find a good reason to change. WHY do you want to be organized? WHY is much more important than HOW you are going to do it. If you can get a hold of WHY, we can teach you how.

Have you ever gotten an unexpected call from out-of-towners in the middle of a lazy weekend?

"Hi! We're up at Burger King on Highway 99 and thought we'd drop in."

Where does the energy and motivation come from as you dart, stash, cram, chuck, and turn your living room into a presentable place to entertain? (We call it the dance of the Seven Disorganized Dwarfs: Dart, Stash, Cram, Chuck, Hide, Hoard, and Stow.) The effort comes from having a very good reason to do it. You don't want casual and nervy acquaintances to think you're a lazy, messy, couch-lounging dog. Because of this, you can muster incredible energy to make the place look good. It sounds pretty stupid, but stupid works!

We used to think that your reason to change had to be pure and good. We now know that reasons don't have to be noble to work. What you have to do is find a reason that will be strong enough to keep you working on the goal.

If you want to lose weight so that you will be healthier, GREAT! But if you're doing it so you'll look fabulous at your class reunion and make your old boyfriend wish he'd never let you go, THAT'S FINE, TOO! If you want to stop smoking so you'll live longer, GOOD FOR YOU! But if you want to kick the Camels so your hair won't stink and your smoke fingers will get their color back, THEN SO BE IT!

If you want to get organized so that you'll be a good example to your children and be a wonderful keeper of your home, welcoming unexpected guests, preparing nourishing meals, and providing an oasis for your family after a busy day out in the world, THAT'S BEAUTIFUL! But maybe you've always felt the condescending, watchful eye of a vicious, know-it-all in-law and you'd like to get organized so you could shove it in her face and show off your pretty, clean, happy, prosperous home, making the stuck-up pillar of perfection so jealous that she would become a binge-eating, rash-scratching, pathetic pile of disbelief. THAT'S NOT PRETTY, BUT IT'S MOTIVATION!

If you've failed in the past to reach a goal, it's probably because you didn't have a good enough reason for achieving the goal in the first place. When we finally realized why we really wanted to get organized, we stuck to our resolution. Looking back, we see that our reason was pretty silly. We both wanted to get organized so we would have more free time to play and not get in trouble with our husbands. We wish we could say that our motives were purely to glorify God and serve our fellow human beings, but they weren't.

Nobody needs to know your REAL reason now. (Once you are organized and have stepped away from the pain of the embarrassment, stress, chaos, anxiety, and guilt this problem usually causes, you might want to share what motivated you ... and then again, you might not.) If you've done some soul searching and you can't find an honorable reason to change, ask yourself for an honest one. If the only way you can succeed is to picture the sneer on someone's face if you fail, then DO IT. If you would like to flaunt the new, financially organized you in front of an old girlfriend or an ex-boss, picture yourself with an expensive leather Hartman briefcase full of money, running past them on Wall Street with a really hot tip and no time to talk. GO FOR IT. Whatever gives you a jolt of energy to pull you off the couch and on to your goal, USE IT. Psychologist and philosopher William James said, "Excitements, ideas and efforts are what give energy."

Famous and successful people have been using creepy reasons to get where they are since the beginning of television (and probably before). Take the famous body builder Charles Atlas, for instance. We have read that he started his early weight training with fear and revenge as his motives. He was a tiny guy who got pushed around by bullies as a kid. He vowed to get strong enough to beat people up if they asked for it. He turned out to be a very nice man and, to his surprise, never had to clobber anybody. We think even a sleazy reason can bring good results. If your reasons are questionable next to a more noble cause, so what? Down the road, when you're healthier, free, and organized, you can do another soul search and move on to a loftier mission.

An interesting thing will happen when you get the results you want, thanks to your secret reason: It will only be fun for a while to rub it in somebody's nose or show off the new you. The longer you live the organized life, the less you're going to care what that original reason was. The truth is that any reason that is less than righteous and good is going to end up like a balloon that slowly loses all of its party air. The old reason that kept you doing a job you didn't want to do will gradually be deflated as you begin to enjoy your new way of life. It is then that a higher purpose will begin to emerge, automatically.

In *The Seven Habits of Highly Effective People* Stephen Covey said that highly effective people know what their calling in life is. He said we need to make a statement (in writing) that defines the calling. He calls it a personal mission statement, sort of like a creed or philosophy that states what you want to achieve, what you want to contribute to humanity, what your character is, and what your values are. He compares it to the Constitution of the United States of America, only it's a personal constitution. Only a highly effective person can sit down and write what his calling or mission is. That's a great idea, but we guess that most of the thousands who bought his book got it because they were NOT highly effective and wanted to become that way.

The thing about missions is that your mission will always be your mission. That will never change. You were born with a unique calling, which was determined the instant all your little chromosomes hooked up with each other. At this point in your life, everything that you have experienced—the joy, the grief, the wisdom, the love, the suffering, the giving—all of it has happened for a reason that has to do with your mission. But that higher calling won't be very clear if you are overwhelmed. It will come to you when you are ... ORGANIZED. Until you are organized, it could be very difficult to write down what your calling is. What is truly wonderful about life is that your purpose will come clear to you when you take care of the little things in your direct circle of control.

Our high calling has been to create happy homes for our families and to use our sense of humor to help people get their homes organized. But back when we were slobs, that higher direction was invisible. If Jesus Himself had come to either one of our front doors in those desperate and depressing days, the encounter would have gone something like this:

Knock, knock, knock?

"Yes? Uh, oh!"

"Pam and Peggy, I am calling you to go out into the world and help my beloved, struggling, disorganized children who are drowning in a sea of clutter, chaos, and confusion."

"Oh, Lord, you have come to the wrong house. You must have meant to go to Nancy's home, two houses down. She is a pastor's wife with five children under the age of five. She is very organized. She's the one you want."

"No, you two are the ones I want."

"But Lord, you haven't seen the inside of our refrigerators."

"Yes, I have, and you're the ones I want."

If you are buried and overwhelmed with your life's circumstances, it would be nonsense to get your personal mission statement down on paper, let alone be ready to receive a commission from Jesus.

That's what we found wrong with most get-organized programs we tried. They were designed by effective people for effective people. They expected us already to be successful and prepared to become even more so.

For now, just get a juicy reason or two, knowing that down the road, when the kitty litter is emptied regularly, when you're not afraid to go to the mailbox for fear it's full of collection notices, when you get to the dentist appointment on time, and when you write letters (and send them) to all the people you owe, the bigger picture will come clear.

STEP FOUR: MEET SCHMIDKY

The fourth step is to meet Schmidky. Schmidky isn't a real person; he's an imaginary character, but he has gotten in the way of our self-improvement by sabotaging our efforts to lose weight, exercise, or stick to a budget. We have discovered that he has a great deal of power in our lives. Since we met him, he has been a major influence in helping us to succeed in areas of self-improvement.

Before we introduce him to you, we want to list a few familiar sayings. No doubt you have heard or said some or all of the following:

I was beside myself.

I was by myself.

I had to talk myself into it.

I asked myself this question.

Part of me wants to do that, but part of me doesn't.

I struck myself funny.

I didn't know what I was getting myself into.

Since the above sentences prove that we talk about ourselves as if we are more than one person, the following shouldn't seem strange.

FROM PAM:

I saw a woman on television who said that she had lost a hundred pounds and had kept it off for twenty years. Although I've never had that much of a weight problem, I have been in and out of Weight Watchers since I had babies, and I wondered how she had kept the hundred pounds off for so long. I bought her book, *Alyce's Fat Chance,* by Alyce P. Cornyn-Selby, in which she explains her theory that we have "internal directors" who run our lives. She says that a person can call on these internal experts to get solutions to problems. I liked that thought, but I didn't know what I was getting myself into when I got quiet and asked to talk to the person in charge of my extra weight. I closed my eyes and pretended I was the mayor of a city that was out of control. In my imagination, I buzzed my secretary.

"Yes?"

"Who's in charge of the intake of food in this place?"

"Let me see, that would be Mr. Schmidky."

"Get him for me."

"Yes, Ma'am."

I pictured myself in a lavish office, behind a big mahogany desk. I imagined the door mahogany, with beautiful carvings and brass fixtures. I pictured the door opening and let my imagination soar as I saw Schmidky walking in. He wore a Hawaiian shirt, shorts, thongs, and a goofy straw hat. He had a tall, tropical drink in his hand, with a chunk of pineapple stuck on the edge. He was about twenty pounds overweight. He resembled John Goodman.

"Mr. Schmidky?"

"Yo, that's my name. Ask me again and I'll tell you the same."

"Sit down. We need to talk."

"Shoot."

"I'm twenty pounds overweight, and it's your fault."

"Hey, wait a minute. I'm not in charge of your mouth. You're the one who opens it and puts the food in."

"Yeah, but you are the one who makes me want the food, and I think you are the one who can help me eat less."

"Yeah? What do you want me to do?"

"Well, for instance, Peggy and I go out to lunch too often. It's really fun, but I'm eating way too much. Today I've decided I'm not going to go out with her, but I need your help, because I'm afraid I'll change my mind when I see her."

"Yeah, I can help you, but you need to know one thing."

"What?"

"The Schmidkys are everywhere. My younger brother Darrel works for Peggy, and unless you tell her what we're doing, Darrel will talk all of us into going."

After my imaginary conversation, I called my sister and told her what I was thinking. She went right along with me and said she'd have a talk with her Schmidky and we'd both have a small salad and an apple for lunch. She called me about ten minutes later.

"Guess what?"

"What?"

"I talked to Darrel and he promised to help me, too. However, once I had the talk, something interesting happened."

"What?"

"I discovered that my Schmidky has a very good friend."

"Who?"

"Truman Conniver."

"Truman Conniver?"

"Yeah. After Schmidky agreed to help, a few minutes later I found myself on the phone with Danny, seeing if we could go out to dinner! I finagled a way to get to eat out after all."

"Well, it's good to know who Schmidky's friends are."

Schmidky is your pleasure-seeker. Everyone has one. Even Ordell, although the things that make her feel good are different. One of the things that pleases her is the superiority of being the first to the curb with her can on garbage day. As an added bonus, there is always the possibility that one of her neighbors will have to chase the truck in her nightwear. When she sees that happen, she gets all dressed up and celebrates.

You know what your Schmidky is doing in your life, because if he's out of control, the effects of his work are on your hips, smoldering in your ashtray, or wrecking your credit. You name it; if it's a problem involving too much pleasure, Schmidky is at the bottom of it. No matter how much damage he has done in your life—whether you're on welfare and it's Schmidky's fault; you need to go through Betty Ford's and it's Schmidky's fault; your clothes and your house smell like the lounge at the Legion and it's Schmidky's fault; you're fat and it's Schmidky's fault— Schmidky is extremely important to you, and he can help you.

If you tell your Schmidky how certain improvements in your life would PLEASE you, you will be amazed at what happens! Once he knows that you are unhappy in any area of your life, and you explain new ways you would like to be pleased, Schmidky will set to work to make you pleased and happy in those ways. The important thing to remember is that *you* are the boss. Schmidky is your servant. It's smart to keep in touch with your pleasure-seeker, because he is definitely a key to your self-improvement. In Chapter 7, we'll talk more specifically about diet and physical fitness.

STEP FIVE: GET A PARTNER

The fifth step is to get a partner. Since we are sisters, we took each other for granted and didn't really emphasize, in our early years of teaching, the importance of having a partner. We now know that our success in conquering our problem and getting control of our lives was mainly because of our partnership. You need a partner, too. In fact, when we run into a student of ours who has fallen off the program, it's usually because she tried to do it alone. Find someone in the same degree of a mess as you are. You will be able to share your successes and your temporary setbacks. Your partner will be your single most valuable asset. We know of some partners who are still best friends after getting organized back in 1977, when we started our outreach.

If you do not have a specific person in mind, such as a friend, sister, or husband, start today to find someone. Put a 3 × 5 on the bulletin board at church, in the post office, or at the grocery store, or hire a pilot to drop flyers in your neighborhood. You could even put an ad in the paper. It could say something like this:

PERSONAL: Help Wanted! Just read *Get Your Act Together!* and need a partner. Mother of three, ready to get organized, seeking someone who would like to do the same. Westridge area. Call 696-4091.

We are as adamant about your having a partner as we would be if we were writing this book about how to conceive a child. YOU NEED A PARTNER!

So now you know why you are disorganized and how it happened. You realize what a wonderful person you are. You are going to get a couple of good reasons to get organized, have a nice long talk with Schmidky, and get a partner.

Now what? Well, we aren't going to teach you anything you don't already know. If we did give you a list of things to do, like fix it when it breaks, return it when you borrow it, and clean it up if you mess it up, you wouldn't sock yourself in the forehead and say, "Whoa, you're kidding? I didn't know I should be doing that! This is great information! Thanks, I'll do it!" The truth is you wouldn't do it, because your brain hasn't been the kind that would help you follow through on things.

Your brain has brought you to this point of being overwhelmed, and it's going to take a bunch of new habits to straighten you out. If we told you to hang up your coat when you took it off, we know it wouldn't come as a big surprise that the coat would look better in the closet than tossed over the couch, with the cat sleeping on it. You have to practice putting your coat away before it will become automatic. It will take a while to program the new habit, but if you've been tossing your coat and everything else onto the couch, the dining room table, the counters, stairs, chairs, and bed for even one month, let alone a lifetime, you must go through tossing withdrawal.

Now you might be thinking, "What's the point in hanging up my coat when the rest of my house is a pigpen?" Hanging up your coat will be one less thing to deal with. If you just promised yourself not to make any more messes than you've already made, things would improve. Start with your coat and stretch from there. "But you don't have any idea what a mess I'm in." Yes, we do. As you'll see in Chapter 2, we've come through the dust of our own pigpens. To us, there is no difference in a big or little mess. If it's a mess that has become a problem, it doesn't matter how it compares to another person's mess. Somebody with an attic full of boxes might be in as much despair as a person who can't walk into his den because of piles. A person with a chronic mess in the trunk of her car could be as frustrated as the one who can't get the car into her garage.

Getting organized is a matter of realizing that the ONLY things that stand in the way are a few silly habits AND the way you've turned the **thought** of getting organized into such a big mountain. Getting organized is not a big deal.

Jesus said, "If ye have faith and doubt not, ye shall say unto this mountain, Be thou removed, and be thou cast into the sea; it shall be done" (Matthew 21: 21).

Two

The SLOB Sisters

From Pam:
My sister and I not only share the same genetic defect; we share the same history of disorderly conduct. We can trace it back to the summer day we moved into the same bedroom. (I get to write this chapter because my recollection of that time is far clearer than hers. I was ten and she was five! For one thing, I remember that the bedroom really wasn't one, and she thought it was. In reality, it was the gutted upstairs of our old farmhouse.)

A piece of plywood almost covered the stairwell hole, except for the last two stairs at the top. Dad had thrown an old tarp over the rest of the opening to seal off the upstairs and conserve heat in the winter. We had been allowed to play up there, but when I asked if we could sleep in the unfinished, unplumbed, and unheated upstairs, I hit a parental cement wall. I spent most of a year in relentless petition and, sometime in early summer, Mom and Dad caved. With the caving, Peggy and I got a double bed, two dressers, all of our personal belongings, and seven years of inspection-free living in that upstairs room.

Our born-organized mom was not willing to lift the ply-wood and the tarp in order to inspect our living quarters. Every morning when we came downstairs, she said, "Girls, how does your room look?"

We said, "Fine!"

Our "fine" and her "fine" were two different "fines."

For those seven years, our mess didn't cause us much of a problem. In fact, we enjoyed a kind of chaotic bliss. We have had to give serious thought to when our organizational defect really started to cause us pain. For each of us, it was when we entered junior high.

In junior high we were hit with our first long-term assignments. We were finally forced to face reality when our teachers began assigning them. They were called units and they had to have maps, graphs, pictures, a table of contents, and a bibliography that was supposed to represent all the research we had done. Since we would usually have six weeks to complete the assignment, this was our first real, hands-on experience with procrastination. SIX WEEKS SOUNDED LIKE SO MUCH TIME!

Our brains have a hard time taking a large project and breaking it down into smaller, manageable parts, so we put off such matters until we were forced to work nonstop to finish the assignment by its deadline. To this day we still have bad dreams, where we're in the classroom and everyone hands in thick, colorful, bound units on everything from Costa Rica to Frog Anatomy, and we have nothing to give but a pile of pretty pictures ripped out of *National Geographic* or some random frog drawings stapled together. The dreams are as scary as any nightmare, and our husbands know how to bring us back gently to the present.

"Babe, wake up. It's just another unit dream. You're big now."

Peggy and I have talked a lot about our "unit dreams,"

and in sharing their horror we have come to realize that the person who is disorganized and out of control is a lot like the alcoholic. The trap begins innocently enough. Remember *The Days of Wine and Roses*, when Jack Lemmon and Lee Remick started out sipping a sweet and tasty chocolate liqueur? Near the end of the movie, they were staggering, slobbering inebriates who had lost everything, including each other. Disorganization starts out innocently, too. You leave the foil from a chocolate Hershey Kiss, with its little paper tail wadded up, on the coffee table, and soon it disappears under a heap of newspapers, junk mail, banana peels, gum wrappers, cups and glasses, magazines, loose change, business cards, dishes, dirty napkins, peanut shells, stray hairs, and nail clippings.

In his book *Choices and Consequences*, Dick Schaefer addresses four defenses that the alcoholic uses to try to change reality and avoid changing behavior: denial, projection, rationalization, and minimizing. You are probably out of the denial stage (refusing to recognize or accept that you have a problem) or you wouldn't be reading this book, but it's interesting to think back to the first time you realized you were disorganized.

I can remember Mom telling us we were a mess, but we didn't believe her. We were like little puppies who played hard and then slept long. Surrounded by love, we had "enablers" like our disorganized dad and Granny, who'd say to Mom, "Aw, c'mon, let 'em play. They're so young and free."

The four defenses came into play with the units. Here's how.

Denial. For me, it started in Mr. Mattenich's seventh grade science class. After a few easy weeks, he hit us with the big assignment.

"Students, we are going to learn about reptiles. Reptiles are in the phylum Chordata. They belong to the subphylum Verbrata, and make up the class Reptilia. You will have six weeks to complete your unit on reptiles. You'll need to spend a great deal of time in the library doing research...."

The next thing I knew, I had a month and a half to research the life of the lizard. I had to find out how he sleeps, who or what he eats, what he looks like on the inside and out, what we as humans use him for, who his enemies are, where he came from, and where he's going. I could not have cared less.

Vicki Schram was excited. "Wow, I'm gonna get started tonight! I'm gonna have my mom take me to the main library downtown so I can check out some great books on lizards."

An alcoholic denies there is a drinking problem. Easily caught up in Vicki's enthusiasm and unable, at the time, to know that I was in DENIAL, I thought, "Yeah, I'm going to start tonight, too!"

With great concern, Vicki said, "Six weeks isn't very much time to get all of this done."

Six weeks seemed like an eternity to me. I thought, "No problem, I've got way over a month." DENIAL!

Vicki's concern didn't fade. "I don't want to let this go to the last minute like some people do."

"Me either," I agreed.

She continued, "If I have to have twenty-five typewritten pages, that's an awful lot of work, especially with all my other classes."

It didn't even occur to me that I couldn't type yet. "Twenty-five pages, no big deal." DENIAL! DENIAL! DENIAL!

Rationalization. Inventing excuses to make unacceptable behavior seem acceptable. The alcoholic might rationalize that everything is under control, that he can quit drinking any time he wants to and that he is only drinking socially. As the weeks passed, I began to rationalize that everything was under control, that I could start any time, and that my social life was far more important than learning about Reptilia.

Two weeks passed; I had done nothing. I watched Vicki Schram's efforts stack up. Her dad even bought her a small lizard, and she had been charting his sleep patterns and eating habits.

Four weeks passed. I told myself that I had two whole weeks left. Vicki's unit was shaping up into something for which the government might pay some serious grant money.

At five weeks, my ability to rationalize kept me from any conscious form of frenzy. After all, I had seven whole days and the whole UNIVERSE was made in that length of time.

Projection. Finding blame with others. An alcoholic projects his problem onto other people and circumstances. Six weeks passed, and the day came when Mr. Mattenich announced, "Students, please turn in your units."

I had cut out a picture of a lizard and copied, word for word, what was written in the "L" volume of our encyclopedia. There was no way I was going to turn in such a disgraceful piece of work. I went up to Mr. Mattenich and, with a heavy heart, I projected, "Margie Vannoy told me our units weren't due until Monday! And every time I went to the library, Tom Prediletto had the 'L.'"

Mr. Mattenich liked me, and he didn't like seeing me so upset.

"Now, now, don't cry. I can give you till Monday."

From after school on Friday night until I caught the bus Monday morning, I worked on the lizard unit. I didn't sleep, I didn't bathe or comb my hair, I stayed in the same clothes, I didn't get to watch TV, I barely took time out to eat. My life was focused and dedicated to the study of lizards ... and everyone in my family was reptilia-conscious as well. I had turned all of them into enablers!

On Monday, I handed in the unit, as promised. It had

twenty-five typewritten pages (Dad did the typing for me). The maps were great (Peggy had colored them with the expertise of a master colorer), the graphs were fabulous, the drawings were clever, and the cover was absolutely Steven Spielberg. Mom had let me cut up an old, fake alligator purse into the shape of tiny lizards. I glued the shells of an open and gutted walnut on the cover and had the lizards coming out of the shells and spelling my title with their little fake bodies ... *Lizards in a Nut Shell.* I got an A.

Minimization. Made to look less serious than it is. The alcoholic minimizes his drinking problem by emphasizing how little the problem affects him. With the A I got for *Lizards in a Nut Shell,* I thought, *"Hah, I got an A for something that I created in two days! Those fools spent six weeks working on their units, and I did mine in a weekend!"*

Using the four defenses didn't stop with the units; they were just the beginning. And just as experts claim alcoholism is a progressive disease, Peggy's and my problem progressed to astounding dimensions. As adults, when faced with vacations, Christmas, remodeling, moving, getting ready for a new baby, income tax preparation, dinner parties, birthday parties, or anything that required a commitment of time and more than one or two steps, we clung to our precious defenses.

I was seventeen when we moved from the farmhouse to the home our parents still live in today. When the plywood and tarp seal was removed, Mom went upstairs and into shock! She was flabbergasted to discover that her "fine" wasn't the same as our "fine."

"It's a ghetto! How in heaven's name could you ever sleep in such squalor?" she shrieked.

Mom struggled to cope with our disorderly life-style after she discovered the room upstairs. At the new house, she separated us to isolate the most Spontaneous, Lighthearted, Optimistic, and Beloved daughter. (We tied for the honor.) In desperation, Mom read a bunch of books on child psychology and found one that dealt with "the messy child." She tried to follow the author's advice and close the doors to our rooms so the chaos wouldn't drive her nuts. According to this book, in time, out of a natural desire for order, we would clean up our rooms.

It never happened. When forced to straighten up or face the penalty of solitary confinement, we'd stash the mess behind our dressers, under our beds, or in the backs of our closets. Since Mom didn't have a "stashing mentality," she assumed that when the room looked tidy, it was. She would stand in the doorway of one of our rooms to make her inspection, and, without suspicion, she always let us go free ... until the next time.

The idea of hanging something up or putting it back in its place was, to us, a complex concept akin to quantum physics. Years later, Mom finally resigned herself to the fact that she had raised not one but two slob daughters, and she regularly apologized to our befuddled and frustrated husbands.

In spite of our cluttered and chaotic childhood, units and all, we still managed to enjoy it. But our lives took a serious turn when we waltzed down the aisle into the real world of marriage, motherhood, and homemaking. It's a cruel awakening for the domestically challenged. A demanding world of in-laws, overdrafts, chimney fires, diaper rash, peeping Toms, door-to-door salesmen, car pools, pets, toddlers, teenagers, and disconnection threats. When we said, "I do!" we had no idea how much had to be done.

In the time it takes to have six children, we did. With each addition to our families, we went further down. Our homemaking was only as good as our resourcefulness. We found that a Cornish game hen would fit nicely inside a turkey if there was no other stuffing available. Late bills could be marked "Please Forward" and, when placed behind the rear tires of the car and rolled over, would give the impression that the already suspect postal service had temporarily lost our otherwise timely payments. Jogging suits could be slept in and, after a couple of days, would make the wearer look like a marathoner.

We became masters at creating the illusion that we were successful homemakers, but all too often our deeds would lead to public humiliation. There was the time the car mechanic dislodged a petrified Big Mac from under the front seat of my car, solving the mystery of why the automatic seats would not work. Peggy still hasn't lived down the time Jeff's schoolteacher made a visit and seated herself on the living room couch. She didn't know that she was also sitting on a couple of Milk Duds. While she chatted happily and sipped a cup of hot tea, the chocolate-covered caramels melted and fused themselves to the back of the teacher's white skirt and the cushion of the couch.

It wasn't as if we never tried to change. Every New Year's Eve we would vow to clean up our act, but by Valentine's Day (as we were taking down the Christmas tree), we knew that, once again, we had failed.

We even bought self-help books, including *How to Stop Procrastinating* (we never did get around to reading it); *Is There Life After Housework?* (there wasn't); *The Time Minder* (we didn't), and *Motivate Yourself* (we couldn't). The problem was that the authors of those books were born organized and seemed to have no idea how bad things can get. A highly effective, genetically organized person could not possibly address the concerns of those of us who struggle just to be minimally effective.

Stephanie Winston, the bestselling organizational wizard, would never wear her husband's Jockey shorts to work as Peggy did. Before she had kids, Peggy worked for *The Columbian* newspaper. The usual backup on laundry often left her without underwear. Whenever that happened, she simply wore a pair of her husband, Danny's, shorts. One day she got caught. Going down the stairs at work, she slipped at the top and bounced to the bottom, where her boss stood in helpless horror.

"Oh, Peggy, are you all right?"

"I'm all right, I'm all right!" She wondered if he'd seen her shorts.

"Well, it's company policy that we take you to the doctor just to make sure you're fine." He was insistent. They went straight from the bottom of the stairs out to the company car and to the doctor. By then Peggy was beginning to feel stiff and sore. An X-ray was ordered.

"Strip down to your underwear and lay on that table," a cranky old nurse ordered. The humiliation of having to lie on a stainless steel X-ray table in a bra and men's Jockey shorts defies comment.

I too suffered humiliation, but more than humiliation, I was in a constant battle with my husband, who was crotchety and demanding. Sometimes he didn't know what went on behind his back. Shortly before I got organized, we moved from Fresno to Vancouver, Washington. We drove a few weeks ahead of the moving van. My husband had told me to get some tranquilizers for the cat, because she hated riding in the car. I had forgotten to get them. Knowing how volatile he could be, especially when I didn't follow through with his orders, I had to make an emergency call on my right brain, when, just as we were leaving, he asked for the tranquilizer. I brought him a capsule. I watched him poke a Dexatrim down our poor cat's throat. During the trip, the cat was a nervous wreck, and she didn't eat for days.

On June 16, 1977, my sister and I both hit bottom. On that day, the Bekins van pulled up and delivered my stuff. I had 157 moving boxes, all marked "MISCELLANEOUS." A load of wash that had been accidentally left in the washing machine had also made the long haul from Fresno. (Mold travels quickly in a hot moving van. All of our clothes, all of our upholstered furniture, and every sheet and towel had a musty smell and a faint green tinge.)

Peggy's crisis actually started brewing the day before. What happened that day is best told in her words.

FROM PEGGY:

I knew it was wrong to go to the zoo with my sister that morning, but I did it anyway. Danny had shown signs that he was close to reaching his personal point of no return. His damp underwear had refused to quick-dry itself in the microwave, and the look on his face, as he snatched the steamy briefs from my hand, had warned me not to speak. Before he left for work, he had questioned me about my plans for the day.

"So, what's on that TO DO List for you today?"

"Uh ... I thought I'd clean up the house and get some groceries."

"Well, wouldn't that be nice, but don't overgoal. Why don't you just concentrate on one thing?"

"What?"

"GET GROCERIES!"

When my sister called to ask if I'd like to take the kids and go with her to see the first viewing of the new baby elephant, I knew I should turn her down. In fact, I did turn her down. "Oh, Sissy, I can't. Danny's all huffed out of shape this morning. We're out of everything around here, and I promised him I'd get groceries today."

"Groceries? So what's the big deal? It'll take us twenty minutes to drive over to the zoo, we'll look at the baby for twenty minutes, and twenty minutes later we'll be home. Let's go! I'll help you get the groceries when we get back."

It sounded so foolproof and deliciously devil-may-care. I couldn't resist. We piled our six kids into her station wagon and headed for the zoo, like a busload of Elks on their way to Reno. When one of our kids asked about dinner, we realized we'd stayed all day. We raced through traffic to try to beat Danny home. There was no time to get groceries, so we stopped at Bill's Burger Bucket for something for dinner. I knew if I could at least feed him, Danny would be pacified enough to discuss the grocery problem like an adult.

My sister pulled up and yelled our order into the speaker. "We'd like three Bronco Burgers, two Chili Bull Dogs, one with cheese, two Double Heifers with extra onions, a Triple Bull Dozer with everything, two large Bucket-O-Fries, seven regular Cokes, two diets, and be quick about it."

"Excuse me, ma'am, we didn't hear that order. Could you move your car up a little?"

My sister, who wasn't wearing her glasses, had ordered into the heat vent! When we got to my house with the burgers, Danny wasn't home yet, but there was a sheriff's car in my driveway, and a couple of my neighbors were standing in my yard. The sheriff came up to the station wagon.

"Which one of you lives here?"

"I do." My voice was shaking.

"Well, I hate to be the one to tell you this, but somebody broke into your house. Your neighbor over there saw 'em go out the back and run down over the hill." We were absolutely stunned with disbelief that anyone would actually do that. We'd seen break-ins on TV, but you never think it'll happen to you. "Just try to stay calm when you go in there, but I gotta tell ya, they ransacked the place ... even ate and left their plates in front of the TV!"

When we went inside, we were pleased. It was exactly the way I had left it. Nothing had been touched. When Danny got home, the poor sheriff was finishing up his report. Danny told him that he thought the reason the crooks didn't take anything was because they were totally confused in there and probably thought somebody else had beaten them to it. For a moment I was tempted to tell

Danny that there *was* one thing missing ... THE GRO-
CERIES!

At that point, I did not know that things would get
worse.

We would have been at the end of our ropes (if we could
have found them.) Each of us had, in fact, been there
many times before, but never both of us on exactly the
same day. On the morning of the sixteenth, Peggy sent
Danny to work with long, gray cat hair covering the back
of his police uniform in a circular pattern that matched
the shape of a baby's behind. Peggy had started to diaper
Ally, their sixteenth-month-old, when the phone rang.
Peggy left Ally on the bed, and when she returned to the
bedroom, Ally was sitting bare, Vaseline-bottomed, on the
uniform that had been laid out while Danny showered.
Peggy flipped the shirt over, and the sticky Vaseline
attracted the cat hair from the bedspread, where the cat
had spent the night. Danny never knew.

He also didn't know that what he thought were the
clean socks he was wearing were really dirty socks sprayed
with deodorant and warmed in the dryer on "high." He
didn't know that his face was tinted a faint shade of
turquoise (since Peggy hadn't gotten groceries, she had
secretly filled the empty Lectric Shave bottle with blue
food-colored water).

Peggy listened as the Smurf-faced crime fighter delivered what she called a "mild ultimatum."

"GET GROCERIES!"

When he left, Peggy, motivated by guilt, started on a
cleaning tangent. Staying in what she had slept in (one of
Danny's oversized T-shirts and bottoms to a pair of his
pajamas, whose top had been lost in the laundry months
before), she started vacuuming. She told her kids to dump
out all their drawers and she'd help them sort and store
their winter clothes. Completely unaware that her right
brain was a ruthless idea machine, she was a servant to

every impulse. She pulled some weeds in the flowerbed, pulled out the contents of the pantry, took down the drapes in the living room, washed two windows, plucked one eyebrow, started a garage sale pile in the hall, wrote part of a letter to Aunt Viv, called Mom, and, at some point, ended up in a tent her kids had made from couch cushions and the drapes she'd taken down.

The doorbell rang. It was Danny's boss. He had dropped by to look at a travel trailer Danny had advertised on the police bulletin board. There was no way Peggy could find the key to show him the RV. There she was at noon, in makeshift nightwear, chicken hair (chicken hair gives new meaning to the traditional "shampoo set," because you shower and wash your hair late at night and then go to bed with wet hair that sets during the night in a style that depends on how you position your head on the pillow— usually the effect is reminiscent of a rooster's topknot), no makeup, 187 pounds, and a house from hell. The boss just backed out the door, giving her a look that she has never forgotten. *"How did Dan get hooked up with a deal like this?"*

After he left, Peggy called me, described what had happened, and confessed how embarrassed she was. I told her about the moving boxes and together we stepped out of denial. On that momentous day, we began our trek from pigpen to paradise. We found out that the journey requires three things:

1. A firm decision to change. (We definitely had that.)
2. A commitment for the right reasons. (We had that, too.)
3. A plan. (That we didn't have.)

We spent the afternoon at a local restaurant, mapping out a strategy and a system. In Chapter 4 we will explain that system, which has evolved over the last fifteen years—

into the perfect tool for sidetrackers as terminal as we once thought we were, to Ordell Daily types who need to lighten up and have more fun in life, and everyone else in between.

The plan involves a new way of thinking, which is just like getting a script for a play. If you were an actress and you were going to play the role of a very organized wife and mother, you would (if you were a good actress) research the character and become very aware of the way organized people act. This doesn't mean we want you to turn into an Ordell, but we do want you to become acutely aware of how she functions, because part of the time you are going to need to act like her.

The best advice we've ever heard, when it comes to learning anything new, is to copy the masters. So, if you wanted to learn to paint dancers, you might study Degas. If you wanted to become a great dancer, you might rent a bunch of Gene Kelly movies. And if you want to clean up your act, you need to mock the masters of order. To do that, we need to take you to Intercourse, Pennsylvania.

Three

Why You'll Never Meet a Disorganized Amish

Intercourse, Pennsylvania, home of many Amish families. There are no disorganized Amish. (According to a library book we checked out, they have a high suicide rate, but none of them is disorganized.) That's because the Amish live very simply, they aren't bombarded with worldly distractions, and their good habits and daily routine are infused into their bloodline. (Perhaps the printed, Monday-through-Sunday underpants were inspired by an outcast, Amish entrepreneur, who grew up with the memorized weekly plan of "Monday's washday, Tuesday's ironing," etc., and could see the need for the world to get on a regular laundry and personal hygiene program.)

The Amish Garden

The simple Amish way of life carries over into every area. Take their gardens, for instance. They never overplant or grow for show. Their neat, tended rows of thriving vegetables are bordered, in moderation, by pretty flowers, whose purpose is not to impress but to distract the bugs. Throughout the community, there are no rambling, weedy patches of overgrown salad fixings that have bolted and gone to seed. Snoopers could not find one zucchini past pan-size, let alone one as big as Schwarzenegger's thigh. There'd be no big, brown tomatos that nobody came back to pick or worm-ridden radishes the size of beets.

Unlike many secular gardeners, the Amish really do reap what they sow. They know their seeds because they gather them by hand from their own gardens when the time is right. They also know exactly how many of them to put back in the ground, in order to get out of it what they need for their table. Since they tend their gardens right after breakfast, they never dig, pick, or pull on an empty stomach. That prevents them from ever scalping their plants, as a hungry reaper might do. Nothing is wasted, and everything is done according to a precise plan, which each family follows.

We, the chronically disorganized, on the other hand, have to be careful of anything that multiplies and has to be tended. We are easily inspired to start new projects, but it's one thing to watch the Master Five-Minute-Gardener do it on cable TV and another to race down to the Rusty Hoe and fly headlong into reckless propagating. Planting on impulse, without thinking of the long-term commitment of a growing garden, is almost as irresponsible as a momentary frolic on the flatbed of a Toyota 4X4. Planting is the easiest part of the growing process; it's the weeding, watering, thinning, pruning, and fertilizing that come afterward that take all the time. The Amish would never let their pole beans choke the tassels off the corn stalks because they had neglected to set up the necessary poles before the teenage seedlings were itchy to climb something and crept into the corn rows. For the Amish, gardens are serious business, and the rules for planting are handed down from generation to generation.

In our second book, *The Sidetracked Sisters Catch-up on the Kitchen,* we warned sister slobs to think before they sowed, offering our own "30 RULES TO GROW BY." Some of the best rules included the following:

Start small.

If you plan to travel, don't plant at all.

Make friends with a farmer and borrow his tools.

If you can't take care of your house plants, don't try a garden.

Be patient and don't pull up carrots to see how they're doing.

Keep deer away by tying your teenager to a post outside your garden when he's been grounded.

The Amish Home

Inside an Amish home, the functional simplicity continues. The purpose of the living room is to accommodate fellow Amish for services on Sunday. Each family takes its turn hosting the regular gatherings and preparing the afternoon meal. Never on a Saturday night would an Amish mom have to fly through the house, tripping over toys and yelling at everybody to pick up their stuff for the next day's meeting. There wouldn't be anything to pick up, because they don't collect STUFF in the first place! She wouldn't have to shriek at her teenager to "Turn down that music and get off the phone!" because there wouldn't be a stereo and there wouldn't be a phone. There'd be no fights over the TV clicker, either. Nobody would have to put the cover back on the VCR or round up the tapes and match them to their jackets. There'd be no need to work at the nail polish stain on the carpet or to haul the piles of old magazines out to the trunk of the car to hide them.

In our slob days, if we had wanted to have a gathering

after church, we'd have had to make a whirlwind swipe through the living room before we left in the morning. (We'd have forgotten the night before that we had invited people over.) Each one in the family would have grabbed a grocery sack and, as if in an Olympic track event, dashed around the obstacle course, bagging up clothes, dirty dishes, newspapers, coffee mugs, slippers, dog toys, stuffed animals, craft projects, and anything else that had been used and left out during the week. Snapping at one another, blaming and making excuses, we'd have left for church in the spirit of anger. Consequently, we'd be nervous, cranky, tired, fighting Christians when the guests knocked at the door for fellowship.

It might be nice not to be invaded by worldly distractions and enticements. There would be no confusion, because you could keep your attention on what you were supposed to be doing. A friend wouldn't call to see if you wanted to go with her to the mall and get a make-over at The Mud Pack. You wouldn't spend time figuring out which shows you'd watch on TV. There wouldn't be commercials to make you feel sorry for yourself, and you wouldn't be tempted by mailers from your favorite department store, luring you into their 15-HOUR LAST CHANCE SALE!

Don't Do It! Don't be snared by materialism and get off the track like Peggy did one year. This is her story, and it contains a warning for other sidetrackers with credit:

FROM PEGGY:

Last year I charged Christmas. I didn't mean to, but as the big day drew nearer, I guess I got sucked into the notion that there weren't enough gifts under the tree. I think I can blame it on television. I saw a couple in a commercial who really loved each other, and, in the end, he handed her a pretty velvet ring box and she teared up and he held her close. You didn't get to see what he bought her, but underneath the frame it said, "Diamonds are forever," so you knew it was something pretty good. Then I saw little children in awe over their toys from Santa. The mom and dad just smiled at them and then at each other, and then the dad pulled out his Discover card and showed it to the mom, and he winked at her like a little elf. They were all so happy.

I left for the mall, armed with a full wallet. I checked my weapon like a gunfighter checking the bullets in his pistol before a shootout. The cash compartment was empty. *Hmm* ... I looked at the splendid, well-stacked row of credit cards, some silver, some gold, some green. Then three things happened. I pictured all the beautifully wrapped packages I could put under the tree, surprising my delighted family. I heard the distant voice of my hard-working husband, warning me to let the Visa cool off. Then I bargained with the credit devil and agreed that I would only use my department store cards. (I had enough of those to get lots of nice things for the people I love.)

Looking back, I wish I had told the revolving Satan to get behind me, but he and I made a pass through the mall that Danny and I would be paying off for months to come. In the spring, when the clothes I'd charged were either outgrown, stained, or too wintry to wear and all the other stuff was forgotten, the bills were still there. I made a decision never to be tempted again. Now, there are no more deals with the credit devil. In the past I had cut up the plastic demons, knowing I could charge without them, using my driver's license as ID. This time, when the bills were paid off, I closed the accounts.

When you're all caught up in the spirit of Christmas, and the commercials are beckoning you to buy, buy, buy, remember that charging your gifts isn't a gift at all. It's a burden you place on yourself, and your family. Remember my words, DON'T DO IT!

In our experience, homes today are overloaded with

things. The objects may be worth money, but, stockpiled, they lose their value. In one home we visited, the couple collected expensive Precious Moments figurines. Each one represented a significant milestone in their lives, but jammed together on three shelves of a bookcase, there was nothing precious about them. In fact, they were depressing. Regardless of whether you're collecting teddy bears, fabric, tools, Tupperware, yarn, magazines, recipes, paints, plants, pictures, or other treasured accumulations, if you can't get to them to enjoy them, how valuable are they?

How much easier would it be to have only what you needed? How much faster could you wash the dishes, launder the clothes, pay the bills, and clean the house if you had to handle only what you actually needed, instead of what you had accumulated?

We found an interesting article in *Money* magazine a couple of years ago, about the American dream. The writer, Walter L. Updegrave, interviewed folks (rich, poor, and middle class) from all across the United States.

A generation ago, the American dream consisted of a black-and-white TV and a basic, eight-hundred-square-foot house with a carport. When summer hit, the family piled into the station wagon, like the one the Cleavers owned, and headed for the Grand Canyon or Yellowstone. When Junior tossed his mortar board into the air, he had just three short months to work to help pay tuition, until he hopped a Greyhound for college.

Today the American dream has escalated into a rat race of cranky commuters, who work fifty- and sixty-hour weeks to finance their sophisticated collection of the latest whatevers. Updegrave writes, "Clearly, the American dreamers of three decades ago reached and surpassed their goals. The past 20 years of progress came with hidden costs, however. To acquire more and better of everything, just about everybody gave up free time and amassed a mountain of debt....

"In the past two decades, much of the stuff of dreams was purchased with the paychecks of hard-working women. In 1989, 74% of women ages 25–54 were in the labor force compared with 49% in 1969. While many wanted careers for reasons of self-fulfillment, most knew they were trading off time and home life....

"Yet the impulse to spend more—largely on conveniences like eating out and high-tech appliances—grew quickly out of the two-paycheck life-style. More begat more. Consumer credit became an addiction. Total consumer installment debt rose from $97.1 billion in 1969 to $716.6 billion in 1989."

What we think is especially interesting, in this conservative, money-oriented magazine, is that when subscribers were polled and asked to rate twenty-four elements of the American dream, the one that came out FIRST was something money can't buy ... HAVING A HAPPY HOME LIFE!

Isn't it interesting that, in our pursuit of happiness, we have ended up charging seven times more than our parents did, to buy the things we think will give us pleasure? In the end, we have had to leave our homes to go to work, to help pay the bills for the happiness gadgets, and then wish, above all else, that home—the place where we don't have time to be—is happy.

Here's a poem Pam wrote that sums up the whole problem.

DISILLUSIONED

I got a job a month ago.
Today's the day they paid.
They took out some withholding
And FICA's got it made.
When I cashed my paycheck
For the thirty days of work,
I went to pick the children up
And nearly went berserk

'Cause when I paid the person
Who agreed to watch my brood,
There was just enough left over
To buy the dog some food.

I thought that when I got this job,
My wallet would be thicker.
I'd ease financial tension
And we'd no longer bicker
Over little things like overdrafts
And disconnected phones.
We'd pay off all our credit cards.
We'd reconcile our loans
On the car we bought in '83
And trashed in '85,
And the one we're driving currently
And hope it stays alive.

I thought that when I went to work
The checkbook would be in the black.
Maybe he'd buy that boat he loves
And I could take a whack
At tennis at the country club,
Where everybody goes.
I'd buy a BMW.
I'd get some classy clothes.
We'd take that cruise to Mexico,
The vacation of our dreams.
We'd leave the kids at Gramma's,
Romance bursting at the seams.

We'd rip up all the carpeting.
The walls could use some paint.
The kitchen needs remodeling;
The sink's my main complaint.
I'd get to buy a stereo

That plays a compact disc.
I'd also get a VCR.
That too is on my list.

The kids don't like the sitter.
My life is in a shambles.
I never see my husband,
And all we eat is Campbell's.

There's never time for romance.
We're lucky if we kiss.
I don't have any leisure.
It's the simple life I miss.

All I ever wanted was
To ease financial stress.
Instead I'm hypertensive
'Cause the house is in a mess.

I guess I was mistaken
By what I thought would be.
There is no extra money,
And there's no time left for me.

The Amish don't pursue happiness; they are in the pursuit of simplicity and Godliness. We admit to a worldly attachment to our possessions, but, inspired by their simple, less-is-better ideals, we have culled the chaff from the treasures worth keeping, and we are happier for it.

We have always admired self-discipline, whether it's shown in athletics, art, religion, or just daily life. While we know we wouldn't be able to live the totally disciplined life of a Mrs. Schimelpfenig in Lancaster County, we can learn from her organized ways. She has dozens of GOOD HABITS, a DAILY ROUTINE, and a WEEKLY PLAN, and we do, too.

Good Habits

It takes twenty-one days to establish a habit in the sub-conscious mind. If you made your bed for three weeks, on the twenty-second day, if you didn't make it, you'd feel as if something were wrong. Organized people, like the Amish, rely on the support of their good habits, and we can, too. We have developed TEN HABITS TO MEMORIZE AND LIVE BY. They are not going to be head-slapping, light-bulb-goes-on, new thoughts, because you already know you're sup-posed to be doing each one. They are old ideas that we'd like you to think about with new enthusiasm. As you memorize them and then act on your memory, think of them as little soldiers, out in front of you, protecting you from feeling like Lucy and Ethel at the candy factory, shoving chocolates down their blouses in an effort to keep up with the pace.

Ten Habits to Memorize and Live By

1. Pick it up, don't pass it up; and don't put it down unless you put it away.
2. Finish what you start and keep the horse before the cart.
3. When you're on the telephone, visiting, or watching TV, do something productive with your hands.
4. If you can't talk and do something productive with your hands at the same time, put masking tape on your mouth and get your work done.
5. Eat sitting down.
6. Make your bed for your own self-respect.
7. Make sure that each room in the house serves its own purpose.
8. Do it when you think of it.
9. Don't write long letters.
10. Work faster; say No when you should and say Yes when you can. Ask yourself, "If I do this, in a year from now, will it matter that I did it?"

Peggy's two sons tell about their experiences during their first year at West Point and the Air Force Academy. When they first arrived in June, they were required to memorize not only their daily routine but all sorts of information (such as the entire front page of the *New York Times*). At first it seemed impossible, but, with practice, their brains accepted the assignment, and by fall, when the academic year started, their lives were on automatic pilot. Memorizing the basics left their minds free to think of more important things, like calculus. The rigorous demands on body, mind, and spirit brought out a slogan one of them coined. Chris said, "I just kept telling myself, 'Let your memory serve you.'"

The Daily Routine

After you've memorized the new habits, you need to memorize a daily routine. Pretend you're an Amish woman. You don't have to start milking cows or churning butter, but pretend you are a very tidy, organized woman who takes care of tasks before they develop into monsters. Draw up a daily routine that such a person would have and memorize it as if you were playing her part on the stage.

If you asked an Amish woman what time she gets up and what time she goes to bed, she'd know the answer. She sticks to her routine like a goldminer sticks to his claim, because she doesn't have to think about it. Everything can be reduced to a habit. As soon as you memorize your daily routine, it will become a habit and everything will have a place in your new schedule.

Sometimes the home front can seem like a battlefield. There is always so much to do and never enough time in a day to get the things done that we wanted to. If we can let our memory serve us, so that a routine is already etched in our mind, we won't have to waste time figuring out where we're supposed to be and what we're supposed to be doing.

A regular routine doesn't need to be scary. It also doesn't have to be a workaholic routine that would make Ordell look like an easygoing slacker. If you've never had a regular daily routine, don't go to extremes with this. Our first attempt at a schedule had us up too early, running too fast, working too hard, and, after three days, swatting at flies that weren't really there. Don't try to be on a fast-tracker's routine if you're a sidetracker by nature.

In the next chapter, we will show you our daily routine, which we put on 3 × 5 cards (see page 59). Before you read further, take some time to think about an ideal day. First plug in all the givens. Those are the things you can't get away with skipping. While you obviously can't figure in the unknowns, you can program the compulsories like eating, sleeping, working, playing, exercising, etc. If you're a night person, arrange your routine to fit your personality. If you're an early bird, give thanks for the gift and figure out the rest of your day. Above all, DO NOT TRY TO GET ORGANIZED WITHOUT A MEMORIZED DAILY ROUTINE AND A WEEKLY PLAN ... IT WON'T HAPPEN!

The 7-Day Weekly Plan

The Amish worked up the singsong limerick that kept them washing on Monday and ironing on Tuesday, etc., and because all the ladies were singing the same song, nobody felt sorry for herself. Since the grass wasn't greener in the other guy's yard, the laundry was done and the homemaker was on to another simple task. We worldly wives and mothers have the challenge of balancing work outside our homes with cooking, cleaning, finances, carpools, children's sports, vacation planning, holidays, and entertaining.

With all the demands on the modern woman, we understand that a simple weekly plan is not EASY to make. In fact, it is the single most DIFFICULT part of getting and staying organized. Most won't make one! Out of one hundred people who read this book, only five will actually take our advice and make a weekly plan. You could be one of the five, if you could just get a glimpse of the magic of it.

Think of a weekly plan as a disposable guide to focusing your life for seven days at a time. When written on a 3 × 5 card, it's also earth-friendly and can be recycled as your situation changes. Above all, don't be intimidated by the thought of failing to actually do what you said you'd do because you wrote it down on paper. If the plan is loose, you can be, too. Basically, we have learned that there are seven different elements to a weekly plan. If one element is left out, the week will be out of balance and so will you.

In a typical week, you will need to devote a certain amount of time to do housework, play, be with your family, rest, run errands, and do paperwork. Your WEEKLY PLAN should include the following:

A Play Day

This is a focus for the day, not an entire day to do nothing but play. Remember the old adage, "All work and no play makes Jack boring," but all play and no work and Jack goes on welfare. A play day is a day in which you have set aside SOME time to pursue your own interests. On this day, your free time won't be occupied doing housework, you won't be going grocery shopping, and you won't be making stew at the rescue mission, unless that is what you love to do. This is a day that has time plugged in for reading, painting, lunching with friends, etc. It's a day in which you set aside some time to refresh yourself—and you must do it GUILT FREE! (If you feel guilty about having fun because you have been accused of playing all the time when there was work to do, don't forget that this is a new plan. Now you will schedule your play and you will deserve to take the time out, because on work days you will have done what you needed to do. Remember, THERE ARE SIX OTHER DAYS TO BE CONSCIENTIOUS ... PLAYING IS GOOD!)

A Desk Day

Of the six remaining days, you will need to select a day of the week to spend time at your desk. That is not to say that on that day you will be strapped to your chair with a pen in your hand for twenty-four hours. (Don't Scrooge yourself on this day. Remember, even Bob Cratchit got to go home at seven.) It only means that you'll spend time paying bills, balancing your checkbook, answering letters, planning family activities such as vacations, holidays, birthdays, etc., making lists, entering contests, reading grocery ads, and clipping coupons that you want to use. In fact, you might want to plan your DESK DAY to coincide with the day your local newspaper features the best grocery ads. That way, you can more easily plan your menus. It won't take an entire day to catch up on desk piles, but it will require some focused attention at your desk. This is also the time each week when you will work with your card file (but that concept is one chapter away). For now, just sketch in a particular day of the week where you will set aside time at your desk. (By the way, if you don't have a desk, GET ONE!)

A Full Cleaning Day

OK, this is the day you work like an ant trying to get a potato chip off the deck and up his hill before it starts to rain. This is a day you'll need an extra swipe of Mennen Speed Stick because, for four to six hours, you are going to be an Ordell clone. Until your house is de-junked (see

Chapter 6), you will spend your cleaning time in the closet. Once everything is streamlined (and we mean 90 percent of the stuff is gone), you won't actually be able to CLEAN. When you have gutted your closets, cupboards, and drawers throughout the entire house, then you can actually spend this time scrubbing and polishing surfaces. You'll see wood look good again. You'll smell the results of Pinesol. You'll marvel at the nap in the carpet and you will Windex your face in a mirror that once looked like a sheet of aluminum. And after you've been a cleaning maniac (and everyone in the house knows it), you'll slump down in a LA-Z-Boy and feel wonderful!

A Half-Cleaning Day

This is a day for general home maintenance on a minimum scale. Without telling you exactly what you should do, let us give you a feeling of catching up, falling back, and regrouping. Take some time (two to four hours) to focus on laundry, dust, pet fur on carpets, toothpaste blobs in sinks, and closed containers in the refrigerator. This is not a day to sweat; it is a day to make the rest of the week run more smoothly. We set the timer at ten-minute intervals to keep us working fast. It's a trick we play on ourselves. Knowing the dinger will go off soon, a latent competitive spirit within takes over and makes us try to beat the clock. Try it yourself. In a couple of hours, you could get so much accomplished that you could relax for the next three days!

A Go-fer Day

On a go-fer day, obviously, you will need the car. If yours is a one-car family, arrange with your spouse to have the car the same day every week. This day is reserved, not for fun, but for buying groceries, banking, going to the dry cleaners, library, hardware store, mall, post office, or anywhere else your errands lead you. If everyone in the family knows you have a specific day to be out on a supply run, requests can be limited to once a week. Remember you're not one of those rubber balls hooked to a paddle by a long rubberband. Don't be thrown out of the house to Lumbermen's for a sheet of plywood, jerked back home, slammed over to Dick's Rent It for a nail gun, bounced back, thrust across town to The Clog Doctor for a plunger, snapped back and whacked out again to the Patch Master for spackle just because your spouse is on his back in the bathroom. Don't let people foul up your weekly plan just because they weren't organized. If a need arises before the go fer day, the needee can do without till the following week or get what he or she needs on his/her own. This only works when the ruler of the weekly plan really does act as a go-fer when she says she will. People love regularity. Businesses thrive on it and so do families. To know that every Wednesday, for instance, is grocery day, is very calming to a hungry teenager and even more comforting to a busy mom, who doesn't need to waste time floundering at an empty cupboard or groping through a 7–Eleven at dinner time.

A FAMILY WORK DAY

With freedom comes responsibility. This is the day when each person in the family can expect to contribute to the maintenance of the household. There might be a lawn that needs to be mowed, a car that needs to be washed, clothes that need to be ironed, or special projects that would take an hour or two of someone's time. Rather than be a martyred mother, working by herself for six hours on the weekend, doesn't it make sense to get everybody to pitch in? If there are five people in the family, everybody could work for an hour and ten minutes and accomplish what one tired female could do in a day. The family work day will pay off unexpectedly when each, in his own way, is proud of where he lives because of what he has done to make his home the best it can be. Teaching children the value of having a good work ethic will serve them for life. Remember that you don't do them any favors when you do all the work yourself.

A FAMILY PLAY DAY

Most people choose Saturday or Sunday, which are our society's traditional days of rest. This is the day that you and everybody else in the family get to be minimally effective. You can sleep late, slop around in your nightgown or pajamas until you feel like getting dressed, and do nothing if you feel like being a zero. You can go to church, take a nap, watch football, or read a book, but, most important, you can do whatever makes you feel rested and refreshed as a family. Part of this day could be devoted to a family activity. Plan to do things together. You're all stuck with each other for a very long time, so you might as well learn to enjoy each other's company. The best way for all family members to appreciate each other is to spend time having fun together.

Take a few minutes to think about an ideal weekly plan. How could you arrange the seven elements of a balanced week into your own circumstances? If you can fit in a scrap of time for each of the seven basics in the next week, you will discover the magic of the weekly plan. Next week it may change. That's OK. That's life! Just get a focus for the next seven days and see how much easier the week is.

When you are outlining the week, don't forget that you have a family to help you get everything done. Peggy's daughter, Ally, who is seventeen, buys the groceries each week. Using a duplicated, standardized list of all the items they usually buy, together they mark the list for the week. Peggy signs a dated check, made out to the Safeway, and writes her driver's license number by the address. Ally cuts out coupons from the newspaper to turn in at the check-stand. Her reward for her time is that she can use whatever money she can get back from the coupons on magazines, makeup, or other goodies. The time and effort average out to be worth about five dollars each week, and Ally has become a very wise shopper!

When you have a weekly plan sketched out, put it on a 3 × 5 card and tape it inside the lid of a 3 × 5 recipe box. The box will become your best friend in the next few weeks, but for now the weekly plan is all you need to put in there. If you haven't made out a weekly plan, you might as well close this book and go back to your old ways, but remember, you could be one of the two who actually gets organized. All you have to do is get a plan!

You don't need to try to be somebody you weren't born to be. It's no coincidence that Providence didn't deliver us into an Amish household or Ordell's kitchen. Our mission in life is clear to us. It is to be lighthearted and happy and to simply live each day so that, at its end, we feel good about what we accomplished or what we shared with someone else. Our weekly plan and daily routine reflect our need for flexibility and our fun-loving natures. They might make Ordell shudder, but the plans work for us because they're a realistic schedule that we know we can stick to or change.

Ring, ring, ring ...

"Mmmello?"

"Hi, Ordell, this is Peggy Jones from church. Your name is on a list I have of people who clean up in the kitchen on Sundays.

"Yes, I do it every first and third Sunday."

"Yes, I see that you have been doing that for the last eight years. I was wondering if you could possibly swap with Esther Higgins and take next Sunday, since she's just had surgery?"

"No."

"Uh, couldn't you just ..."

"Peggy, dear, I don't SWITCH anything EVER."

You will find that this 7-day plan will honor your gifts of flexibility, spontaneity, lightheartedness, creativity, love of living, and optimism. By honoring those attributes, it will be much easier to stick with this new way of life and change it whenever you want to.

F o u r

It's in the Cards!

Working with the cruel genetic hand we've been dealt, we have learned to happily play the game of life in nervous remission and win. And thanks to that shaky state, we have stayed on the cutting edge of self-improvement movements, in search of relief for ourselves and our disorderly brothers and sisters. Breaking free from disorganized bondage ourselves, we know what will work and we know what won't.

In the fifteen years we have been teaching household upkeep to the downtrodden, we have honed our advice to the very simple rescue plan we are about to outline. It took more than a decade of trial-and-error experiments to come up with just the right dose of direction a person needs to get it together. When birth control pills first came out, the heavy dose recommended was enough to sterilize a hippo. Today, medical science has learned that only a fraction of the prescription is necessary. Over the years, we have proved that the same thing is true of our formula for good housekeeping. Our advice has changed dramatically, as we've learned more about the psychology of getting and staying organized. Like the birth control pill of the sixties, the early card file system we were on was an overdose of discipline that few sidetracked people could survive. Today, we have reduced the prescription and we take it ONE DAY AT A TIME.

FROM PEGGY:

Back in 1977, when we were trying to make sense out of our chaotic lives, Pam was surprised to learn that I had been very organized at one time in my life. Never at home, but during the five years I worked at *The Columbian*, before I had children, I was a pillar of order. The top of my desk was a clean sheet of metal each time I stepped away for my lunch hour. At night, when I left my cubicle, it was as if I had died and someone had cleaned my desk in anticipation of hiring a new employee who would come and make a reasonable mess. My fellow workers joked about it because it was odd. They didn't realize how afraid I was to leave one scrap of paper, for fear I'd disappear in a mound of unfinished work. I forced myself to stay on top of things, because I knew my tendency to procrastinate, and I NEEDED the job to help my husband get through college. I got in the habit, right from the start, of keeping my desk perfect, but each night I would leave my controlled environment at the office and step into the reality of a home fit for swine. In 1977, when my sister and I got our homes organized, I know my co-workers at *The Columbian* thought it was a scam. On the surface, anyone would have thought I was a compulsive organizer instead of a scared slob trying to cope in the working world.

In examining why I could have been so organized when it doesn't come naturally, I realized it was because there was already a system in place. Because I mind really well, all I had to do was learn the routine and establish the habit of leaving things neat.

At *The Columbian*, it was my responsibility to get advertising from businesses. Regular advertisers wanted an ad in the paper every day, while others wanted one every other day, weekly, monthly, or just occasionally. Rather than work from a master list, we used 3 × 5 cards to keep track of the clients. On each 3 × 5 we put the name of the business, address, phone number, person to contact, and how often an ad was to appear. Inside a card file box there were dividers for the days of the week, as well as monthly dividers. We always kept the current day in the front of the card file; all of the businesses that were scheduled to be called that day were filed in front of that day's divider. After the call was made, the 3 × 5 card was refiled so that it would reappear on the next day that the business had to be called again, depending on its advertising frequency.

As I thought about the simplicity of that system, it occurred to me that HOUSEWORK IS REPETITIVE—at least if you do it and then do it again when you're supposed to! Housework could be put on 3 × 5 cards just as advertisers had been. With that one idea, Pam and I revolutionized our housekeeping standards. Today, we have streamlined our own card files and will share with you some new things we have developed to make them serve our needs even better.

Think of the box as your housekeeping command center. It will contain all the central intelligence of your home. Inside, you'll need a small calendar for the year, similar to the kind on the back of your checkbook register. You'll use the calendar to schedule future activities, such as making Halloween costumes, decorating for the holidays, planning vacations, or working on income taxes. You'll want to tape your weekly plan (you know, the one you made after reading the last chapter) into the lid of the box for easy reference.

Next you'll need to purchase some dividers. Get Monday through Sunday dividers to schedule daily activities, and put them in the front of the box. Use January through

December for less frequent activities, and put them behind the days of the week. Then get a package of alphabetical dividers and put them in the back of the box. They will serve as your reference section for frequently used phone numbers and addresses, as well as a cross-reference for items you file in folders in your bigger filing cabinet later. Get rid of your ugly old address book and transfer the current, up-to-date addresses and phone numbers to blank 3 × 5 white index cards, using one card per address. We don't use address books anymore because people move and the pages get messy. If you buy a new book every few years and transfer everyone over, it is time-consuming and unnecessary. In a purse-size daily planner, which we replace at the beginning of each year, we copy just a few names, addresses, and phone numbers we might need when we're away from our card file. (Eliminate names and numbers magnetted to the refrigerator or scribbled on the cover of the phone book.) Finally, purchase some blank dividers to keep track of information regarding special interests such as gardening, camping, entertaining, etc., and label them accordingly. Mark one of them "STORAGE," so that items you pack away when you clean out your closets, cupboards, and drawers can be catalogued and kept track of on a 3 × 5 card in the back of the card file (more on that in Chapter 6).

With the basic parts of the card file set up, you will be ready to make out the cards. Although this is time-consuming, it will be the key to unlocking the door of organization and stepping into a smooth-running home. Originally, the only cards we had were work cards, and they got old fast! We also had too many of them because we put only one job on a card. Now, after fifteen years in the box, we've realized that that was unnecessary. If several jobs in one area have the same frequency, we put all of them on one card. That means fewer cards to handle and keeps us focused in one place. The biggest change we've made since we developed our original system is the addition of some cards that make life more fun! We'll explain that kind in detail in a minute.

To start using our new system, you'll need to fill out six different kinds of cards, not counting the cards you'll use for addresses, storage, and special interests. (We use six different colors of 3 × 5s for each category, but that's up to you.)

ACTION CARDS

Action cards are a pleasant way to say "work cards." In this category we have eight 3 × 5s that deal with the kitchen, one with the living room, family room, and dining room, three with the bathroom, two bedroom cards, two laundry, and four miscellaneous cards. Each card follows the same format (see example). We put the frequency of the "action" in the top left-hand corner (daily, weekly, every other week, monthly, seasonal, every six months, yearly) and the total time estimate in the top right corner. We have estimated, for instance, that we spend thirty minutes every day doing routine kitchen cleanup. On that card six jobs are listed:

Daily	30 Minutes
1. Empty Dishwasher, Set Table.	5 Min.
2. Fill Dishwasher.	As you go.
3. Pots, Pans, Serving Dishes— Hand Wash.	10 Min.
4. Clean Countertops, Surfaces.	5 Min.
5. Scour Sink, Empty Garbage.	5 Min.
6. Sweep Floor, Shake Rugs.	5 Min.

Sample action card.

Kitchen

When we began the system, we thought housework took much more time than it actually does. When we finally got around to doing it, we were so far behind that everything took longer to finish. Cleaning the kitchen when you haven't tackled it in a while takes a lot longer than doing it every day. Instead of a sink full of pots and pans to wash, you'll have only a couple. Because you know what needs to be done, you'll be able to delegate jobs to other family members.

The cards need to be typed so they don't have the personal implication your own handwriting would have. Your handwriting insinuates that you are the boss, telling someone else what to do. Typewritten, the action cards are the impersonal, factual reality in black and white that there is lots of work for everyone to do.

Continue to make out your kitchen ACTION CARDS, including a one-hour weekly or every-other-week card with the following jobs:

1. Wash the Window over the sink.   5 Min.
2. Clean the Refrigerator.   10 Min.
3. Clean Microwave.   3 Min.
4. Clean Range Top.   5 Min.
5. Wash Floor.   15 Min.
6. Wax Floor.   15 Min.
7. Self-cleaning Oven.   5 Min.
8. Wash Scatter Rugs.   2 Min.

Of the remaining kitchen ACTION CARDS, five will need to be done every six months. We group them in the following way: On one card put:

1. Wash Canisters, Knickknacks.   5 Min.
2. Clean Cutting Board with Bleach

(Then Put in Dishwasher
if It's Plastic). 5 Min.
3. Clean Small Appliances. 5 Min.

The total time estimate is fifteen minutes. At the bottom of a card like this, we put the words "Last done," with a space for marking, and "Skipped," with another space for the date so that we can keep track of jobs that have to be rescheduled. If any card comes forward to the current day with two skips logged, it becomes a priority action and must ACTUALLY be addressed before it can be refiled.

You'll also need a separate card that directs you to "Clean, Reorganize the Pantry." This will need to be done every six months, with a time estimate of one hour. In addition, make out two more cards marked "Clean, Reorganize Cupboards" and "Clean, Reorganize Drawers" (each job will take one hour). Each of these kitchen jobs will also need to be done every six months. Finally, every six months you'll find this kitchen card:

1. Clean Light Fixtures
(Put in Dishwasher). 15 Min.
2. Clean Stove Fan, Filter, Hood. 30 Min.
3. Wash All Kitchen Windows. 15 Min.

Once yearly you will have a card that tells you to:

1. Defrost Freezer 55 Min.
2. Clean Drip Pans, Coils
Underneath Refrigerator. 5 Min.

You can see that, when done routinely, all the kitchen jobs can be staggered so that your kitchen always looks good and never gets out of control or becomes too big of a job.

You'll need one card to take care of the basics in the

living room, dining room, and family room. We group those rooms together because they need to be cleaned weekly. If everything is already picked up (which it will be if you play the infraction game you'll learn about in Chapter 11), all you will really need to do weekly is vacuum (ten minutes each room) and dust (five minutes each room).

There are only three bathroom cards to make out. One you'll do weekly or every other week, with a time estimate of forty-five minutes. The jobs include:

1. Clean Toilet	5 Min.
2. Clean Tub/Shower Stall.	10 Min.
3. Scour Sink.	5 Min.
4. Clean Mirror.	1 Min.
5. Polish Counters.	2 Min.
6. Wash Floor.	10 Min.
7. Wax Floor.	10 Min.
8. Wash Scatter Rugs.	2 Min.

The other two bathroom cards have a seasonal frequency. Each card will take one hour of your time.

1. Polish Woodwork.	20 Min.
2. Polish Tiles.	20 Min.
3. Clean Light Fixtures.	10 Min.
4. Wash Windows.	10 Min.

The second card will have you:

1. Clean, Reorganize Cupboards.	30 Min.
2. Clean, Reorganize Medicine Cabinet.	30 Min.

That will take care of cleaning the bathroom!

Next, make out two separate bedroom ACTION CARDS.

One will be done weekly or every other week and will take about twenty-five minutes. You'll need to:

1. Change Sheets.	5 Min.
2. Clean Under Bed.	5 Min.
3. Clean Mirror.	5 Min.
4. Dust.	5 Min.
5. Vacuum.	5 Min.

The second card will need action seasonally. It is part of the deep cleaning that will take about two hours.

1. Turn Mattress.	
2. Wash Mattress Pad, Bedding.	5 Min.
3. Clean Closets, Drawers.	45 Min.
4. Clean Fixtures, Lamp Shades.	10 Min.
5. Wash Windows.	30 Min.
6. Blinds, curtains, etc.	30 Min.

There are only two laundry cards. One is to be done daily, with an actual time estimate of fifteen minutes per load of wash (the number of loads per day will depend on the size of your family):

1. Sort into Three Baskets (Darks/Blues,Other Colors, Whites).	
2. Wash, Dry.	5 Min.
3. Fold, Put Away	10 Min.

Note: Laundry must be sorted in the morning before anyone leaves the house. Levy an infraction penalty (see Chapter 11) for laundry left in bedrooms or sorted improperly. The last laundry ACTION CARD will take thirty minutes each week and includes:

1. Mending.   10 Min.
2. Ironing   10 Min.
3. Hand Washables.   10 Min.

Laundry only becomes overwhelming when it's left undone. Do it regularly when the card comes up in your card file and you can handle it easily, with cooperation from your family (more on that later).

The remaining action cards fall into a MISCELLA-NEOUS category. Three cards are to be done weekly. The first is miscellaneous pet care and requires approximately fifteen minutes to:

1. Change Kitty Litter   5 Min.
2. Clean Bird/Hamster Cage.   5 Min.
3. Other pet cleanup.   5 min.

The other two weekly ACTION CARDS will take considerably more time. One card will show up on your scheduled "desk day" and you will need to plan on spending about two hours finishing it. You will:

1. Plan Menus.   10 Min.
2. Make Grocery List.   10 Min.
3. Clip Coupons.   10 Min.
4. Sort, Answer Mail.   30 Min.
5. Pay Bills, Balance Checkbook.   60 Min.

The other miscellaneous ACTION CARD will also take about two hours and will probably be handled on your "Go-fer Day." On this card, type the following activities:

1. Miscellaneous Errands—time varies.
2. Banking.   10 Min.
3. Post Office.   10 Min.

4. Dry Cleaners.   10 Min.
5. Wash car, clean inside.   20 Min.
6. Grocery Shopping.   45 Min.
7. Unpack Groceries.   15 Min.

A final miscellaneous ACTION CARD will need to be scheduled seasonally so that you:

1. Clean Fireplaces.
2. Clean Furnace Vents (put in dishwasher if they fit).
Both jobs will take about one hour.

That takes care of all the housework you'll ever have to do in a year. If you cover the 3 × 5s with clear contact paper, they will be plasticized and will last forever. You can mark notes on them with a washable marker or use Post-it notes for comments or reminders. In all, these twenty action cards replace the old version of the system, which had you handling more than a hundred cards. We think the simplified card file will be easier to use and will keep you on track and help you stay focused.

Midway in our organizational odyssey, we realized that all work and no play made us mad. Aside from the ACTION CARDS, we suggest you make out "extra credit" 3 × 5s in the following categories: REFLECTION CARDS, REMINDER CARDS, FLASH CARDS, ROUTINE CARDS, and our favorite, REASON FOR LIVING CARDS.

REFLECTION CARDS

These are cards to add to your card file to help you relax. We've found that, in our busy lives, we all need to take some time to think about our blessings and our accomplishments and to focus on a positive attitude. Reflection not only brings a great sense of inner peace; it also reinforces new habits while helping you let go of the old. If your church puts out a

monthly meditation booklet, you might not choose to copy
the thoughts onto cards, but we have found that paraphasing
a particular selection, writing it down, and putting it in the
card file makes it more personal and deepens the meaning
with each reading. Choose a number (thirty-one would give
you one reflection card per day for a month) of special quotes,
Bible verses, sayings, or profound thoughts to read and think
about each day. Whenever you have a quiet moment, at bedtime, for example, select one. Read it a few times and focus on
the message. Then, the next morning, read it again and try to
live the theme of that reflection card for the entire day.

MY GOALS

I know where I am going. My path arches high. The spectrum
of my experiences will give me strength and purpose. Life will
guide me toward what truly fulfills me. Each moment in time
moves me closer to the completion of my journey toward success. I know what I plan to do. It is already an accomplishment
in my inner experience. My actions are a simple projection of
my inner design. Already certain of the outcome, I am able to
adapt to any cloud of gloom or fear of doom. Eagerly I set out
on my life's journey

Sample reflection card.

REMINDER CARDS

These bold little gems (use a wide felt marker) remind us
to do the basics. We suggest you post these reminders in
strategic places where you tend to get sidetracked. For an
example, we have several cards that say, "Don't Do It!" We
have one on the refrigerator to stop unconscious eating, one
in our purses to prevent impulse buying, and another by the
phone, to cut down on long-distance calls.

The following are suggestions for additional reminders.

ORDER NOW!*

*This is a reminder to keep things orderly. We post it in places where we could be tempted to leave a mess.

EVERYTHING WILL BE ALL RIGHT!
(This is a nice card to run into if you tend to worry a lot.)

SPEED IT UP!
(We have a tendency to move too slowly, and this card reminds us to move faster.)

SOMEONE MIGHT DROP IN!
(This is not meant to be a stress-inducing card. It is an energy-creating tool to remind you that you could have some unexpected company, and you'd want the house to look nice.)

RELAX AND TAKE A DEEP BREATH!
(When you run into this card and do what it says, you'll be surprised at how tense you were.)

FLASH CARDS
Flash cards have a "buzz word" on one side and a rule to memorize and live by on the other. Until we knew

them by heart, our card files included the following flash cards:

Buzz word	*NOW*
Rule to live by	DO IT NOW.
Buzz Word	*FINISH*
Rule to Live By	FINISH WHAT YOU START BEFORE YOU START SOMETHING NEW.
Buzz Word	*SET*
Rule to Live By	SET A TIMER AND WORK FAST.
Buzz Word	*JUST*
Rule to Live By	JUST DO IT.
Buzz Word	*WRITE*
Rule to Live By	WRITE SHORT LETTERS AND MAIL THEM.
Buzz Word	*SHOWER*
Rule to Live By	SHOWER, DRESS, HAIR, AND MAKEUP BEFORE ANYTHING ELSE.
Buzz Word	*FUNCTION*
Rule to Live By	EACH ROOM IN THE HOUSE HAS ITS OWN FUNCTION.
Buzz Word	*EAT*
Rule to Live By	EAT AT THE TABLE.

DON'T

Sample flash card, front.

DON'T OVERBOOK YOURSELF!

Sample flash card, back.

Buzz Word	PRODUCTIVE
Rule to Live By	WHEN ON THE PHONE, VISITING, OR WATCHING TV, DO SOMETHING PRODUCTIVE WITH YOUR HANDS.

Buzz Word	PICK
Rule to Live By	PICK IT UP. DON'T PASS IT UP, THEN PUT IT AWAY.

If you did nothing more than work your FLASH CARDS, you would have peace in your home as you have never known before!

ROUTINE CARDS

Memorize the following:

MORNING DAILY ROUTINE

Get Up on Time.
Personal Grooming.*
Make Bed.
Empty Dishwasher.
Eat Breakfast.
Follow Your Weekly Plan.

EVENING DAILY ROUTINE

Happy Hour.**
Eat Dinner.
Dinner Cleanup.
Free Time with Family or Alone.
Turn on Dishwasher.
Personal Grooming.
Private Time in Your Bedroom.
Lights Out on Time.

---

*Good grooming may be so basic to you that you don't need to write it down, but from our experience it wasn't that automatic. Including it in our memorized daily routine ensured that we wouldn't get sidetracked and forget how important it is to look your best.

**We don't mean "cocktail time." We'll explain what we do mean, later.

REASON FOR LIVING CARDS

Ah, yes ... the Reason for Living cards ... they are the fiber of life that holds the card file together and makes you want to open it again! In all, there are sixteen golden cards to get up for each day. Eight cards will show up daily in the card file, one will appear three times in a week, and seven more once a week.

DAILY

20-SECOND KISS

A marriage counselor told us that a 20-second kiss can improve an already good marriage. The rule is that you must kiss and not come apart for 20 seconds.

We suggest the following daily REASON FOR LIVING CARDS:

TIME ALONE: (choose one)

Every day you need at least an hour of time by yourself. It doesn't have to be all at one time. Some suggestions of what to do with your time alone are: read, pray, daydream, write in your journal, take a bubble bath, nap, walk the dog, mess around in the garden, enjoy a cup of tea, etc.

TIME TOGETHER: (choose one)

Meet your spouse for lunch, dinner out, a movie, a walk, a picnic, happy hour, singing, etc.

INDULGENCE (choose one)

This is a reward card. (It may be used daily; however, do not give yourself the same reward each day or you will get into trouble.) Go out for lunch, order something out of a catalogue, buy a magazine, have breakfast in bed, go off your diet, call long-distance, get a massage, etc.

GOOD GROOMING

Shower, hair removal, deodorant, dress (all the way to shoes), teeth, hair, lotion, perfume, fingernails, and toenails. WOW!

20-SECOND KISS

A marriage counselor told us that a 20-second kiss can improve an already good marriage. The rule is that you must kiss and not come apart for twenty seconds, twice each day.

HAPPY HOUR

At the end of the work day, you and your spouse need at least a half hour together to relax, talk, and regroup. It's best to have something to occupy the children so your time is uninterrupted. Serve hors d'oeuvres and something refreshing to drink.

FAMILY MATTERS: DAILY

Every day the family needs to share a meal together so that each member can enjoy the benefits of having a close family. Make a list of fun things to do together and pick something from that list each day.

The next card will come to the front of the card file three times each week.

EXERCISE

Experts claim that we should do aerobic exercise at least three times a week and for at least twenty minutes.

Be sure it is something you enjoy. Walk briskly, bicycle, swim, jog, ski, dance, do step aerobics, etc. JUST DO IT!

The seven remaining REASON FOR LIVING CARDS will show up once a week, and include the following:

SELF-IMPROVEMENT

Spend at least an hour a week on personal growth. Study, take a class, read, increase your vocabulary, grow spiritually, work on faults, strengthen virtues, practice something to perfection, go on a diet, etc. All self-improvement takes planning. If you stay in the card file each day, you will be able to schedule the time it takes to be successful.

HOME IMPROVEMENT

Spend at least an hour a week on a home improvement project. Pretend you are going to sell your home or have a big party. Fix all of the things that usually get fixed only for someone else.

PUBLIC SERVICE

Volunteer at school, do church work, or be a political supporter. Open your home (once it's under control) to a child in need, visit the sick or elderly, make dinner for somebody tired, teach something you know, etc.

CHECK NEXT MONTH

Place this card in the weekly dividers on your desk day. It will always be there and, on the last desk day of the month, it will remind you to check the next month's divider for special events you don't want to miss, such as birthdays, anniversaries, etc. You will also find your occasional ACTION CARDS and will be able to incorporate them into your weekly plan.

TIME WITH A FRIEND

If you have a partner who is getting organized with you,

you can team-clean your homes. Exercise together, lunch, shop, etc.

FAMILY MATTERS: WEEKLY

Have a family meeting to delegate work, set goals, plan vacations and holidays, and discuss problems that come up during the week.

After you make out all of the cards, put all of the "Dailies" in front of today's divider. File the Weekly cards, according to the kind of activity they are, to coincide within your Weekly Plan. If any of the tasks on your printed cards will be done less than once a month, file them in front of the appropriate month in the January through December section.

Each night before bed, put the ending day's divider behind, and the next day will come forward. We like to take a look at the various cards that we will need to handle the next day. We put the cards in a flexible order so that we will do the most important things first. Then, depending on our situation at the time, we will either do them, or, if unexpected interruptions occur, we will reschedule them for another day, if necessary, marking them to reflect that decision.

People always ask us how we handle interruptions. Interruptions are a regular part of life. They will hit you whether you are organized or not. If you're using the card file, you merely change direction, and know that you are not neglecting things, you're only adjusting your schedule to fit reality.

Have fun setting up your 3 × 5 command center. Play with it and adjust it to fit your personal circumstances. Put your spouse and children in there. Fill it with your interests as well as your responsibilities. Orchestrate it so that work and play are in harmony with one another, and the card file will become your most valuable helpmate.

Fⁱve

Pigtales

One day a couple of years ago, Elaine Veits, a syndicated columnist for the *St. Louis Post-Dispatch*, called our office to get some spring cleaning tips for her column. Since we had written three books on how to get organized, it wasn't unusual to get a call like that. We were both happy to help her, only not in the way she thought we would.

"I haven't read any of your books, but several of my readers have recommended them, and I wondered if you could share some of your spring cleaning advice with us?"

"We don't spring clean," we said in stereo.

"Really?"

"No."

"I was always told you had to spring clean if you were a good homemaker."

"No ... that's a carryover from your great-grandmother's time when they used coal to heat their homes," one of us explained.

"Really?"

"Yeah, the houses back then were closed up tight through the fall and winter, and a sooty veneer gradually coated everything. In the spring, she *had* to open up the house and clean the scum off her stuff. Today we have what we call electricity and natural gas, and we have yet to find a coat of electricity or a film of natural gas on anything."

"So if you don't clean in the spring, what do you do?"

"Play, mostly. Then we clean in the fall after the kids go back to school and routines take over where the summer slough left off."

The silence was broken with our suggestion. "You know what we could help you write about in your column?"

"What?"

"Well, spring is one of the best times of the year to catch a slob. They sorta come out of their holes, like ground hogs in the spring, to get a breath of fresh air and see what's going on out in the world. You can usually spy one with a new jogging suit and shoes, starting what she hopes will be a regular exercise regime, which will probably last a couple of days."

"That's interesting. I guess I misunderstood what your books are about. I thought, since they were on home organization, you'd be efficiency experts."

"Did you know we're reformed slobs?"

"No."

"We're actually deficiency experts, and we could help you find a slob in your city and do a make-over on him or her."

"A slob search?"

"Yeah, we did one in Detroit and the results were amazing. Just write in your column that you are looking for the messiest family in St. Louis. Have your readers send photos and tell what's wrong with their house and why they want to change."

"What would the winner get?"

"We would come to St. Louis on a clutterbust and actually go to the home of the winner with our weekend recovery program."

"They'll actually have their house clean by the end of the weekend?"

"Oh, no, they'll do most of the work after we leave. The weekend recovery program is an intensive, personalized in-house meeting to map out stategies and teach the principles of our system. In return for our services, the winner would have to be willing to subject the family to the public humiliation factor. They'd have to let you, and a photographer from the *Post*, come with us to record the devastation. In six weeks, you'd go back and document the miracle transformation!"

"Transformation?"

"Yep! All we need is a weekend."

"Who'd be willing to come out of the closet and open their private lives to a huge newspaper?"

"We would've."

Elaine was intrigued by the whole idea of finding and reforming a slob in St. Louis. She couldn't resist the temptation of a make-over on her turf. She couldn't deny that a potential Cinderella story would have definite human interest, but she really didn't think she would tempt many messy contestants. That's because St. Louis is probably the worst place for an organizationally impotent person to live. Elaine told us that a large portion of the population there is known as the "Scrubby Dutch." The Dutch are famous for their cleanliness. They have Dutch Boy Paint and Dutch Cleanser named after them. We know why other countries haven't come out with paint and cleaning products in their names; the Scrubby Dutch have mopped up the market. There's just no room on the shelves for Bedouin Boy Paint or Bulgarian Cleanser.

You don't have to live in St. Louis to know a Scrubby. They stand out across the country as tense, ultratidy people, with a single mission: to glorify their persnickety existence and make the rest of us feel inferior. Their lawns are flawless, their homes are fastidiously maintained, their cars are preserved like museum pieces, they never sit down and nobody else in the family does either. If you live in St. Louis, where there's an infestation of smartalecky treadmillers, you have our condolences. To the rest of you with dirty genes, be thankful you only have to hide your affliction from a few.

Elaine had wondered if neighboring, rubber-gloved Scrubbies would intimidate the slobs of St. Louis and keep them behind closed drapes. Eighty desperately disorganized people wrote in. More than one third of the entrants' letters arrived the day of the deadline. Elaine extended it to accommodate the pathetic stragglers. Another ten came in under the extension wire, and letters and photos continued to trickle in long after the contest was over. (Those were the ones who really needed help.) Think, if eighty were willing to go public, how many shy slobs just wished they could enter, but didn't have the nerve.

Since we live in the state of Washington, we had to help Elaine pick the finalists over the phone. She called after she had waded through and eliminated fifty of the pleas for help. Her voice had lost its lilt. She was depressed.

"I do not know what to do! I was up past three in the morning, reading all these incredible letters. I have narrowed the entrants to thirty-something, and I don't know how we can pick just one."

We asked her to read the ones she'd picked. When she finished, we could see why she was so depressed. It was extremely hard not to be able to help every one. These people were all wonderful! They were great writers, with humor pouring out of their pens, pencils, and crayons. The photos were priceless. They revealed the awful truth about the bedlam that disorganization breeds. These people were so eager to receive help that they were beyond worrying about shame.

Elaine was relieved to learn we had some rules for elimination. For instance, we won't work with whiners. We can spot one in just a few sentences. They're the people who sound like John Candy when he whines. A whiner usually makes a comment like, "Well, it may work for you but ..." We know from past experience that you cannot change a whiner's "but ..."

Once we had a woman in one of our six-week seminars who continually interrupted the lecture with, "But I've got twins!" After three weeks of hearing, "But I've got twins," we were determined to put a stop to her whiny complaints. We called Karen Anderson, who lives near us. (Maybe you've read about Karen; she is the mother of quintuplets and has been written about in many women's magazines.) We asked her to come to our group and talk about how to be organized when you have FIVE babies. Karen is very organized, and we thought that her testimony would shut up the mother of twins. Not so. She continued to whine her way through the entire six weeks.

Another letter writer we eliminated was the person who loved telling all her stories. There was no doubt that the material was great comic work, but when the letter went on for six pages with joke after joke, we could see that the writer would be lost without her material.

Also, some people may really be ready to change, but circumstances and timing are not on their side. Anyone with a new baby should wait at least until the baby is through nursing before trying to reorganize her household. The mother needs at least a year to feel like herself again, and the baby requires so much of the mother's attention in that first year. (That's not to say the child won't also need it in the next twenty years.)

The other reason for eliminating entrants was the severity of the problem. Since we are not psychologists and are not schooled in helping people with BIG problems, we could help Elaine see that the woman who had an alcoholic husband, a child on a respirator, a mother with Alzheimer's and had herself undergone three surgeries in the last year was not someone we could help ... not now. Still, it was agony to narrow the remaining thirty down to one ... in fact, we couldn't. We picked eleven.

The letters that moved us were both humorous and sad. Letters like the one from Kathy, a mother expecting her second child:

Dear Elaine,

Please, please, please pick me! I'm at the end of my pregnant rope. The baby is due in two months and everything is in chaos. I almost had a miscarriage the other day. I thought I saw a mouse shoot out from under the bed and run across the hardwood floor in the master bedroom, but when cornered and inspected, it turned out to be a rather large cockroach caught in a dust ball! I've got to get organized. My husband is a lawyer and he said he would be willing to quit his practice and let me go back to my career (I was a very organized secretary) if I thought that would make me happy, but it wouldn't. I love my home and I love being a mom, I just don't know how to get control of everything and I feel so guilty that I am teaching my young son to be a slob.

Kathy was among the eleven finalists.

We decided to conduct a personal interview with the remaining eleven and then whittle them down to five. Out of the five, we would pick a winner; the other four runners-up would get to go to the house of the winner as observers. It gave all five women a built-in support group, which enforces our advice to get a partner (which, by the way, if you haven't ... PUT THIS BOOK DOWN AND GET ONE!).

When Elaine called the eleven finalists, four had second thoughts and decided not to remain in the contest. Out of the seven who said they'd meet us at the paper for the final interview, only five showed up.

The St. Louis Five

It was a Saturday morning in April. The tension was high as each finalist in the disorganized contest was checked at security and led into the conference room on the second floor of the *Post*. We sat with Elaine on one side of a large conference table. The contestants all had the same comment: "I hope I win ... I think." We passed around the photos they had sent with their letters, so that each one was able to see that she was not alone. They also could see how close the competition was.

Elaine spoke: "I have to tell you how impressed I was with your letters. You all need to know that Pam and Peggy picked each of you for several reasons. It was obvious by your letters that you are basically happy and healthy individuals having trouble with organization. They tell me that you can lick the problem this weekend. I wish each of you my best."

We had the women tell a little bit about themselves and their families, and each of them won our hearts. They were all so sincere about changing. They'd had it with their old ways, and their excitement about the real possibility that their lives were about to change drastically put magic in the little conference room.

KATHY

Kathy was quiet and rather serious. She was thin, except for her huge tummy, which gave the impression that her baby was due any minute. We were concerned about timing, but she assured us that she had well over two months before the baby was due. She told everyone the cockroach story, and, with the laughter that followed, her seriousness disappeared, revealing a very lighthearted, fun-loving mother who wanted more than anything else to be in control of her life.

DEBBIE

Debbie was also very serious ... at first. She told us that she had always wanted to be organized, but somehow it never worked. She said that for Christmas her husband gave her organized closets. He hired a bunch of people who came into her house, built closet organizers, and arranged everything for her. It took under a year for a miscellaneous array of junk to be on the floor, stuffed in drawers, and crammed under beds. Her guilt level was off the meter. She hated that her two sons were following her example.

CINDY

Cindy was a natural comedienne. She told the group that getting organized was a matter of life and death! She had contracted food poisoning from eating a salad tossed in bottled dressing (from her refrigerator) dated for expiration two years earlier. When she was well enough, she went through all the other bottles and dumped five outdated dressings. She, too, had two children and felt guilty that she was such a crummy example for them.

JEAN

Jean had moved nine times in fourteen years of marriage, and each time she thought she would get organized. It never happened. She had a cooperative husband and two children, ages seven and ten. She talked of piles on top of piles and said that when she wrote the letter to the newspaper, she lost it and had to write it again.

PATTI

Patti was a vivacious southern lady with four small children. Her youngest son was ten months old. She wailed about the clutter of toys, clothes, and papers. She and her family were very active in their church, and she confided that she had never been able to invite anyone over from their church on the spur of the moment.

We could see that it would be impossible to choose a winner. There was no way we could pick one over another. We decided to pull the winner out of a hat. Patti won. An hour later we had caravanned to her beautiful home in a lovely neighborhood. On the outside, Patti's house looked fabulous. The yard was beautiful. A weeping willow added to the peaceful setting. On the inside, it looked as if Hurricane Andrew had had his way with her.

There is something magic about getting seven happy-go-lucky, organizationally impaired people together in a mess. It seemed we'd all known each other forever. There was not an iota of judgment in any of us, and Patti was amazed that she felt no embarrassment. Elaine was so devastated by the condition of Patti's home that she turned gray and had to take medication for a migraine. What we learned that day was just the start of our advanced study of the Spontaneous, Lighthearted, Optimistic, and Beloved. Since the St. Louis slob search, we have had the privilege and honor of being invited into more than thirty messed-up homes across the country. We needed to go into about ten different houses before we could perfect our message. The priceless knowledge we have collected will truly change your life.

Six

One Man's Junk
Is Another Man's Junk Too!

Making house calls and conducting "clutter intensives" has given us privileged information. By actually going into homes and getting to see into every closet, cupboard, and drawer, every basement, garage, and attic, under every bed and behind every cornered piece of furniture, we are this country's number one authorities on housebreaking the disorganized! The stashes we've discovered, squirreled away, behind those closed drawers and secret hiding places is the main reason any home is in a mess. The clutter factor in your home is in direct proportion to the state of your closets, cupboards, drawers, and hiding places. If you want to get and STAY organized, the starting place is there.

Before we tell you what to do, we have to harp on the partner issue, just in case you haven't found one yet. YOUR PARTNER IS GOING TO BE VERY IMPORTANT IN WHAT YOU NEED TO DO NEXT.

All the homes we've visited have shared one common denominator: TOO MUCH STUFF! We've been in a mobile

home, a large five-bedroom home in a prestigious neighborhood, an apartment, a teeny-weeny house in the city, a
teenier, weenier house in the country, a mansion, and
many typical, three-bedroom ranchers. We have helped a
senior citizen, a single mom, large families, small families,
and extended families, and we've seen the same thing in
every case: TOO MUCH STUFF! In our dog days, we knew
we needed to get organized, but we didn't realize, in the
beginning, how much we had to get rid of. Now we know
that in every disorganized home, there beats the heart of a
little pack rat. In all thirty homes, 90 percent of what they
had, had to go!

One of the thirty messy winners had enough Tupperware under her kitchen sink and in her cupboards to serve
twenty families. (We loaded her van with the plastic
hodgepodge of containers and took them to her church for
its rummage sale.)

Then there was the "cliptomaniac," who had clipped
coupons and newspaper articles (to read later) until we
couldn't see the furniture. (We arranged to have 1,500
pounds of paper removed from her living room so that she
could reclaim it as a functional room.)

You might not hoard newspaper clippings or Tupperware, but maybe it's pens, fabric, coupons, knickknacks,
books, or one of a million other things. Whatever it is, if
the thought of getting rid of 90 percent scares you, don't
panic. We will talk you through letting go, just like in the
movies, when they nudge a virgin paratrooper out the
door at ten thousand feet. It's not easy to let go of the
things you've collected, but you CAN do it. The reason it's
hard to let go is because, behind everything you have
saved, there is the thought that someday you will need it.
In the process of letting go, we hope to convince you that
you DON'T need and WON'T need most of what you
THINK you need.

The Spark

With every woman we have helped to face the clutter culprits, it has been most exciting to see her sense of humor kick in. We call it "the spark," and we have seen it ignite in all but one. (The one out of thirty who didn't spark really wasn't ready to let go. Every slip of paper and scrap of fabric she threw away was pure agony for her.)

GREAT-GRAMPA TUBERLY'S SILVER

In your mind, you probably can't see that cleaning out your drawers could ever be FUN or FUNNY, but we've found it to be exactly that. In every home, the homemaker, flanked by the two of us, has experienced intermittent hysterical laughter! We didn't know that would happen. We had one of the best times with Cindy. She was organizing her kitchen and, in the back of one of the drawers, she found a bunch of tarnished silverware, wrapped up in a plastic bag and secured with a rubber band.

"Oh, that's Great-Grampa Tuberly's silver. He was a silversmith!" She was proud and we were impressed. She watched us take off the rubber bands and unroll the plastic to expose five blackened silver-plated forks, three spoons, and a couple of knives. Upon close scrutiny of the flatware, we looked at each other, just a little puzzled.

"Sissy, doesn't this pattern look familiar?"

"Yeah, it's just like the ones we had when we were little. Mom got it by saving Betty Crocker coupons."

Cindy protested, "No, it can't be! Great-Grampa Tuberly was a silversmith, and he created his own patterns." She picked up a knife and took a closer look. "Hey, there's an 'F' engraved on this." (Her name started with an "S.") Her memory kicked in. "Wait a minute, Great-Grampa Tuberly wasn't a silversmith, he was an engraver, and not a very good one at that!" She started laughing. "I remember my aunt telling me a long time ago that he was full of it and dumber than cheese. All these pieces have an 'F' on them! This was probably one of his botch-ups, and all these years, I've been carting these stupid things around, thinking they're sterling, family heirlooms."

You are going to be able to do the same thing Cindy did with Great-Grampa Tuberly's Oneida. You are going to look at each and every thing in your possession with new eyes, and through the eyes of your partner, and you are going to see how silly it is to let manufactured goods come between you and your peace of mind.

Looking with New Eyes

For a minute, pretend that you are going on vacation and you get to stay in a very ritzy, four-star hotel. Picture being led to your very expensive and fabulous suite. Think of how wonderful it would feel to walk into your suite, where everything is streamlined and beautiful. The beds are made, the towels are fluffy and white, the decor is tasteful and classy, and there is an air of freshness and freedom. NOTHING is messing up that picture, because you haven't been in there yet. Think how inviting that vision is!

Now imagine having the bellman unlock the door, and the same suite is heaped with everything that is cluttering your home right now! The beds aren't made, there's a load of towels to be folded on the couch, the drapes are hanging crooked, and the TV is blaring. Has your picture lost its glamour?

If you walked into a hotel room that was full of your junk, you probably wouldn't want to stay there on your vacation. It certainly wouldn't be relaxing, and you probably wouldn't be willing to pay to stay there, either. Think how your belongings have devalued your fantasy!

They are cheapening your reality in the same way!

These trappings you think you have to have are causing arguments, tension, lost time, money, peace of mind, confusion, distraction, guilt, chaos, and disorder, just to mention a few of the problems.

In the past, you've probably said something like: "I'm gonna pick this place up!" What you really do when you straighten up the place is move things around. You migrate the piles to another part of the house, or bag or box the piles for a later time. It hasn't worked, and it never will work, because a pile migration always comes back in the spring or sooner.

Instead of rearranging your clogged-up closets, cupboards, and drawers and nook-and-crannying things from one room to another, we want you to try a NEW way.

Organized from the Inside Out

The first thing you need is a timer. You can use the one on the oven, as long as you'll be able to hear it when it buzzes. You need a timer because you are only going to fight this war one hour at a time. You need to think of this process of elimination in terms of time. We can look at a room or a whole house and calculate how much time it will actually take to reclaim it and put it in order. We've seen five-hour living rooms and twenty-five-hour living rooms. The house we found that needed the most time was a three-hundred-hour house with a forty-hour living room. Over a year, that's still less than an hour a day, with one person working. One family we helped was willing to cooperate with one another, chipping away at their two-hundred-hour house, and they had it perfect in three months.

Can you take a guess how many hours your home is going to take to reclaim? In our first book, *Sidetracked Home Executives*, we said, "It's the trend that counts. You didn't get into the mess overnight and you are not going to get out of it overnight." What's the rush? We can tell you what we think the rush is; you want results instantly. That's our Western culture's way. We've been programmed to go for instant mashed potatoes instead of mashed from scratch. (In fact, our kids actually prefer instant to scratch.) Our microwaves, Polaroids, touch-tone phones, remote controls, cruise controls, and all of our finger-on-the-button technology have given us more time. Yet the main complaint you hear is, "I don't have enough time!" Well, we DO have enough time if we will just stop and organize it.

If your home is a one-hundred-hour home, it took you and your family one hundred hours to get it into the condition it's in. AS SOON AS YOU CAN ACCEPT THAT IT DOES NOT MATTER HOW MANY HOURS IT IS GOING TO TAKE TO FIX THINGS, YOU ARE READY TO CHANGE.

Be a Little Bitter

Our idea of becoming a little bitter does not mean to be resentful or begrudging; it means to be able to do a little bit at a time, every day. To be a little bitter, you have to stop looking at the whole picture and stop feeling overwhelmed. You are not a quarterback who's been sacked; you're a wonderful person who has let things go for a while. That same "while" is waiting for you to take things the other way.

We received a call from a woman in tears, who confided that her basement was totally full. She said the stairs were even gone. When we told her to put the timer on for an hour and follow our rules (below), she said, "An hour won't do anything." An hour of work on a mess is an hour of work on a mess. If it was a two-hour mess, true, the hour would take care of half of it, but with a two-HUN-DRED-hour mess, the hour of work wouldn't show. That doesn't mean it's a wasted hour.

With weight loss it's the same thing. If you were one hundred pounds overweight and you lost five pounds, it would not show. If you were ten pounds overweight and you lost five pounds, it would show. And yet there is no difference between the first five pounds and the latter five pounds. Sheryl Pridmore, a friend of ours in Detroit, said, "If you have a sand pail full of sand and you take a cup of sand out, it'll show. But when you have a whole beach of sand, one cup doesn't make a difference that shows." Still, a cup of sand is a cup of sand.

If you have a lot of work to do, you've got to grasp the idea that IT DOES NOT MATTER IF IT DOES NOT SHOW. IT WILL IN TIME!

How to Fight the War on Clutter

You will need the following items, which we will explain in detail:

Timer

Produce boxes

Shoe box

3 × 5 scratch pads

3 × 5 index cards

Pen

Piggy bank

Manila file folders

Cute mending basket

Containers with lids (about the size of a Sucrets box)

Card file

Start by setting your timer for one hour. We suggest starting in the kitchen. The kitchen is probably the room you and your family spend the most time in, so it very well could be a depressing dump site. The best place in the kitchen to start is the junk drawer by the telephone. Take the drawer out and turn it upside-down on the floor or on the counter, or onto a table (if there is room). Once the drawer is gutted, wash it out with detergent and place it back in its frame.

The next step is crucial. THINK BEFORE YOU FILL YOUR DRAWERS! Think about what you have to have in the drawer by the phone. We suggest the phone book, a pen and 3 × 5 scratch pad, Scotch tape, scissors, and fingernail care supplies. (Caring for your nails is a great thing to do while you're on the phone.) You also need to know that you don't have to fill your drawers. Less is better.

The next step involves using your thumb and forefinger of the hand you use the most, plenty of thirty-gallon garbage bags, and three produce boxes (ask the produce manager at your grocery store what day most of his produce comes in and start collecting orange or apple boxes). Don't settle for any medium-size box. Produce boxes are always the same size, making them easy to stack. They're made of extra heavy cardboard. They have holes for ventilation, lids with handles, and they are always available.

Mark one produce box "Give Away/Sell"; one "Put Away"; and one "Storage." As far as your thumb and forefinger are concerned, you need to use them in conjunction with one of the rules we asked you to memorize in Chapter 3: *Pick it up, don't pass it up; and then put it away.* When we say "away," we mean put it in one of the three produce boxes or into a garbage bag. You will have to make one of four decisions once your thumb and forefinger have successfully picked something up.

"GIVE-AWAY/SELL"

The produce box marked "Give Away/Sell" is for items that have value, but you no longer want them in your home. Great-Grampa Tuberly's silverware went into that box at Cindy's house. Make a decision before you start clearing out your house; will you be giving away or selling your unwanted, but still useful, junk? If you decide to give those items to the Goodwill or Salvation Army, just box them up and make a weekly run to their new home on your Go-fer Day.

If you want to have a garage sale and sell all of it, you need to price each item as you pick it up. Have a roll of masking tape and a pen handy so you can price as you go. We have seen too many mythological garage sales. If you merely pile without pricing for that someday sale, you will slowly turn your garage into an unprofitable warehouse of cullings, because the job of pricing will be too much trouble.

"STORAGE"

Things like holiday decorations, seasonal clothing, or anything you will need later, but do not want in the main living area of your home, will go into the produce box marked "Storage." (We'll tell you how to set up a storage area later in this chapter.)

"PUT AWAY"

The produce box marked "Put Away" is for items that go somewhere else in the house. This box will keep you at the job site for the entire hour. When you pick something up, like a videotape, instead of taking it to the family room where you would end up watching it or you would start organizing your videos, just put it in the Put Away box. When an hour of de-junking is up, it will take approximately ten minutes to put away everything that you put in the box.

The **shoe box** is for photos. Collect them in the shoe box and write on a piece of **3 × 5 scratch paper,** "organize photo albums." Put the memo in your **card file** to do ten months from now. You'll also use the scratch pad to list supplies you will realize you need to buy, such as batteries for the smoke alarms, tape, drawer organizers, etc. Keep a 3 × 5 scratch pad by every phone, in your purse, and in the back of your card file. The pads are cheaper than 3 × 5 index cards and can be thrown away once you take action.

The **piggy bank** is for all the money you will find. The **mending basket** will have thread, scissors, glue, etc., and since it is decorative, it can stay by the phone. You'll find lots of things that need to be fixed. Put them in the mending basket and fix them while you are on the phone. The **small containers with lids** will keep items such as safety pins, rubber bands, and paper clips organized.

Write on a **manila folder,** "Desk Day." When you find letters that need to be answered, bills that need to be paid, or anything involving paperwork, put it into the Desk Day file folder, and once a week, on your Desk Day, take time to attend to your paperwork.

We have discovered that there are some things that everyone seems to hang onto, so we have made these very specific rules about what you may keep.

PAM AND PEGGY'S MOTTO FOR UNCLOGGING CLOSETS, CUPBOARDS, AND DRAWERS: *If it's something you haven't hooked up, turned on, eaten off of, covered up in, sat in or on, looked out of, at, or over, mailed, watered, or read in the last year ... dare to dump it!*

The items below are some of the typical drawer, cupboard, and closet cloggers that seem to be universal.

MAGAZINES

Ask yourself this question: When have I ever had a block of free time and used it to scrounge through a mountain of old magazines in search of some old information? If the answer is NEVER, ask yourself this: Will I ever take one of my old magazines with me to the doctor or dentist so I can read mine instead of his? If the answer again is NEVER, then you just might want to follow our rule for magazines.

DO NOT KEEP OLD MAGAZINES! If you subscribe to a magazine or magazines, you may keep only this month's and last month's issues. You may also keep any old, but special, Christmas issues. We know how hard it would be to dump all those commemorative magazines you've saved. It would be cruel to insist that you toss *Life: The Year in Pictures 1985, People: The Royal Wedding Issue*, etc. We only ask you to be very selective.

While you are bundling up the collection of unread material, consider how much of it you have really read. If you see that you have not been reading what you've been paying for, you might consider canceling your subscriptions and buying a magazine only when you know you will have the time to enjoy it (like on a vacation).

If we still haven't convinced you to chuck your treasury of periodicals, remember that there will ALWAYS be more magazines and they will ALWAYS come out every month. If you are afraid that someday the monthly flow of type will stop, remember that there is a place in your town where all the issues of all the magazines are kept, and you can go there, at no cost, and ask one of the professional keepers of information to help you dig out any issue from any year ... it's called THE LIBRARY.

NEWSPAPERS

Our rule for keeping newspapers is simple: DON'T! You may keep one to start a fire in your fireplace. Exception: If you have a teenager who relies on the newspaper for current events and school reports, you may keep back issues for one week only.

KEYS

When you clean out drawers, you are going to find keys, and you will get to keep some of them. Ask each key this question: Are you a key to the present or to the past? If it's a key to the past, and you've forgotten what hole it goes to, throw it away. You may keep all keys to the present.

Keys to the past include: any key with a symbol of a past car you have owned (what are you thinking? *"Maybe someday I'll find my old car and rip it off"*?); any key that seems vaguely familiar but you can't remember what it unlocks; any key that you haven't the foggiest idea what it ever went to; and luggage keys. (If you didn't lock your luggage on your last trip, throw away your luggage keys. If you do lock your luggage when you travel, those keys will be with your luggage and not at the bottom of your underwear drawer.)

Keys to the present include the key to your house, car, office, and anything else you know you'll need to get into. You may discover duplicates as you clean your drawers. They are good to keep in case you lose the originals.

PENS

Test every pen by scribbling in a circular motion on a scratch pad. If scribbling won't release the ink, throw the pen away. You know how hard it is to read a message that is gouged into paper with the inkless point of a dead pen. If ink comes out with the test, it's a keeper. Remember, every pen you find that works is one more pen you can put in the drawer by the phone, eliminating, once and for all, the frantic search for a writing utensil at message-taking time. Also, we caution you not to take pens from hotels. They have only enough ink for a night or two, and you will soon discover a multitude of drained instruments in your drawers.

The typical family is allowed to have a maximum of twenty-five pens.

INSTRUCTION MANUALS

Throw away your instruction manuals to simple appliances like toasters, blenders, mixers, and coffeemakers unless you think you are going to forget how to use them. Keep the rest in your filing cabinet.

TWIST TIES

If you have a surplus of twist ties, it means one thing ... you are not using them. Since you are not using them, why are you saving them? When you buy a quantity of garbage sacks, there will always be enough twist ties to seal each bag. If you are not using the twist ties, it's because you are filling the bags too full. If that's the case, and we think it is, you need a daily card to remind you to empty the trash before it overflows. You may keep six twist ties and make a conscious effort to use them. (Peggy has a twist tie fetish and insists that you may keep six ties in ALL of the various sizes.)

COUPONS

Dump all the coupons in your drawers, because they will have expired. If you find any coupons with dates more than a year old, you lose your cutting privileges until your whole house is streamlined. And don't be fooled into saving a coupon just because it's worth more than fifty cents. Five dollars off a pizza you needed to order two years ago is no good.

Paper Grocery Bags

Keeping grocery bags is very dangerous! We have discovered that they have babies while they are under the sink and in between the counter and the refrigerator. We've been told that in some climates these paper grocery bags also attract cockroaches (they love the glue), which is another reason to avoid collecting them. Because they attract bugs and have a sneaky reproductive spirit, we suggest that you keep only five at any one time. If you feel anxious at this thought, try to recall a time when you had to bring your groceries home without a sack because your grocer ran out of them. As long as you need groceries, you'll get another bag. Many environmentally conscious people are investing in reusable net grocery sacks for small purchases and larger, grocery bag–size sacks are also available in some places.

Receipts, Check Stubs, Bank Statements

We asked a friend who is a certified public accountant how long we should keep receipts for tax purposes. She said that the IRS can audit your files for up to three years unless they suspect fraud, at which time they can ask for your books up to seven years. Since you are the only one who knows if you are frauding, you will have to decide if you will save your papers for three or seven years.

Boxes You Think Will Make Good Gift Containers

If you have a special place to save boxes, you may keep a few. Just remember that with every gift you buy, you can ask for a perfect, new gift box and usually get one.

Odd Socks

Odd socks are like lonely hearts; they need mates, and they won't find them as long as they are shut up in the odd-sock drawer. Free them so that they can get out and meet all the other odd socks in the world. To borrow words from a famous odd-sock song from *West Side Story:* "There is a place for us ..." That place is the Goodwill or Salvation Army. Incidentally, we called the Goodwill to see if they want odd socks and they said yes, but they also wanted us to know that they don't try to mate them. Instead, they use them for various stuffing projects, in which they need fiber in rather small pieces. Bag up all those odd socks you keep thinking will one day miraculously find their long-lost partners ... because they NEVER will.

Souvenirs

If you are sick of your home being a national gallery for the cowboy boot ashtray from Phoenix, the ceramic beaver made out of Mount St. Helen's ash from Washington, the mock leather moose from Yellowstone, and the tin Trump Tower bank from New York City, box up the vacation flashbacks in one of those gift boxes you don't get to keep anymore and pick some lucky guy out of your phone book to receive some unexpected tourist trap mementos. Imagine how surprised the recipient will be when he receives the anonymous, tasteless gift! It would be great if the surprise could arrive on April Fool's Day. Note: In your future travels, purchase souvenirs that can be hung on your Christmas tree. Then every Christmas, when you haul out the fake holly garlands to deck the halls, you'll be able to relive your bygone vacations.

Batteries

Chances are your bevy of batteries is worthless. We all

have a tendency to save them too long. Somewhere in our brains this message is engraved: BATTERIES NOT INCLUDED—so we buy too many in the first place, not wanting ever to be stuck with something new but powerless. It's easy to end up with the wrong size, and there's nothing more frustrating than trying to fit a "C" battery into a double-"A" hole.

Give all your mystery batteries to someone with a tester and, in the future, buy only what you need, and get the kind that come with a little tester strip on the side.

PACKAGED PARTS

These are the little screws, nuts, and bolts that manufacturers so kindly include with new products. These little packages live on long past the time you'll ever remember what they go to. Dump them! In the future, write on the package what the parts belong to and put them with the tool box.

MAPS AND TRAVEL BROCHURES

Maps get outdated, because new roads keep being made. If you find a map that is frayed on the folds and threatens to fall apart if you open it, it's time to throw it out before you get lost. When you plan a road trip, buy new road maps. You'll save yourself time and maybe even gas money in the end.

SAVED "FOR GOOD"

If you keep things for good, be sure you can define what "good" is. We have a friend whose aunt saved all gifts of new clothing for "good." When she died, her closets, cupboards, and drawers were jammed with things for "good." Our friend told us that her aunt always wore the same thing at all family gatherings and that she would consent to wearing something new only when what she had was literally in rags. She was laid to rest in something she'd saved "for good."

SENTIMENTAL THINGS

As long as your sentimental possessions are organized, you can keep them. Plan to organize photo albums, put home movies on video, bronze the baby shoes, make scrap books, etc. Memorabilia is wonderful when it is organized and depressing when it is not.

GAMES

Weed out games. You don't need Candy Land if your youngest child is sixteen. Have a closet shelf for your games and keep only the ones you play with regularity. Games with missing pieces are useless. Most games have the manufacturer's name and address somewhere on the box. Plan on one of your Desk Days to get missing parts to those games you dearly love.

CRAFTS AND FABRIC

Like grocery sacks, crafts and fabric multiply. One of the women we've been helping with her home is a very talented craft person. Her home has a wonderful, cozy feeling, due in part to her gift for decorating. However, her craft room was out of control, and she was almost afraid to go in there. We helped her organize shelves and drawers, and she gained the courage to give up over two thirds of her material. Now she has just exactly what she wants in the room.

Remember that crafts are always changing. If you do crafts, you know that cows are IN one year and mushrooms are IN the next. There is nothing more depressing than to have to finish last year's clown when everybody else is doing ducks. Be brave. Get rid of the old so that you can make room for the new.

Kids' Schoolwork and Art

The papers that your children bring home from school are enough to pack the average household. You may keep only 10 percent of the best work. Each of our kids got one produce box filled with their favorites. The rest was discarded when the little ones were not looking. The box will go with them when they leave home.

Undeveloped Film

Peggy used to have a huge salad bowl on top of the refrigerator, full of undeveloped film. She had written on each cartridge what year and for what event the snapshots were taken. She and Danny would occasionally get the big bowl down and look at the rolls. "Oh, Danny, look, Grand Canyon 1974, Chris was two. I'll bet these are good."

Our rule is, if you aren't developing, you don't get to shoot. Picture taking is a four-part process. Buy the film, take the pictures, develop the film, and put the pictures in an album. Leave any of the steps out and you will be frustrated. If you find a lot of undeveloped film, collect it in a plastic bag and, every Go-fer day, get one or two rolls printed.

Beware of the Phantoms

Without exception, we have discovered phantoms living in people's houses. We even found them in our own houses years after we reformed. We can guarantee that you'll find phantoms in your house, too. As long as you are aware that they exist, you can catch them and kick them out!

We first became aware of the phantoms after a clutter-bust in Sacramento. We came home feeling very good about the condition of our closets, cupboards, and drawers and our ability to maintain streamlined and efficient homes. Peggy even looked under her kitchen sink with a profound feeling of superiority, and that's when she discovered the first of several phantoms we have since rounded up and kicked out.

FROM PEGGY:

I looked under my sink and reveled in the cleanliness and order I had maintained over many years. A garbage can, lined with a plastic liner, was on one side and a Lazy-Susan, with liquid detergent, dishwasher detergent, scouring pads, and a sponge was on the other. Upon further inspection, I noticed, in the darkened recess of the cupboard, another Lazy-Susan that was hiding behind the one holding my dishwashing necessities. "Hmmm ..." I pulled it out into better light.

The turntable was dusty and so were the indoor plant products on it. Leaf Shine, African Violet Food, Vita Root, Blossom Boost, Mr. Mister, "Your Fern's Best Friend," and two different kinds of bug spray. As I looked at the products, I thought, *I don't use any of this stuff*. That's because I'm not good with indoor plants. The ones I have would live regardless of human attention. Why did I have all those greenhouse supplies in the back of my cupboard?

I remember buying all of it when I was at the mall with Mom. She even had two-for-one coupons for some of it. That's how I ended up loading a cart full of horticultural supplies. She was so excited to be saving, and I got caught up in her enthusiasm. I offered to pay half and we'd split the take. I spent about thirty-five dollars on the phantom horticulturist living under my sink. It was me thinking I could grow like my mom.

After discovering this space-taking figment, we uncovered a phantom gourmet who went to The Kitchen Kaboo-dle and bought bundt pans, ravioli presses, and an espresso cappuccino maker. We also exposed a phantom painter, intellectual, athlete, letter writer, and quilter.

When you pull the plug on a phantom, you free yourself to be who you are. Maybe you thought you'd use that yogurt maker, but if you haven't cultured in the last year, you're not going to. Maybe you used to quilt, but you little-stitched yourself into burnout. Pass on the frame and the squares. Times change, you change, and what you keep in your home should reflect who you are now. Let someone else be who you used to be. Face the fact that you can't be all the people you admire. If you keep the phantoms, you hold back opportunities for others to have what you don't need anymore.

Establishing a Storage Area

There are certain things in your home that are seasonal, such as holiday decorations, ski clothing and equipment, and hunting and fishing gear. Clothing, for most parts of our country, is seasonal. As parents of a growing family, you will need to keep things like diapers, potty chairs, and car seats until you have finished having children. These storage things need to be out of the mainstream of your household until they are actually going to be used.

Choose a storage area in the basement, garage, attic, spare bedroom, or any place that is dry and warm. The more organized your storage area is, the easier it will be to get to things when you need them. Our system requires about twenty produce boxes, a divider in your card file marked "Storage," and blank 3 × 5 index cards.

Start by filling a produce box with a specific category of things like "size 12 boy's church clothes." As you put the boy's dress shirts into the box, write on a 3 × 5 card, "3 dress shirts." When you put the sport coat in the box, write, "navy blue sport coat, size 12" and so on until the box is full and you have recorded everything that's in the box on a 3 × 5 card.

Put the lid on the box and mark the outside "C-1," for clothing, box number one. On the 3 × 5 card write "C-1," and put that card into your card file with the divider you marked "Storage."

It's as simple as that! When you have finished boxing up and writing down everything, you will have saved yourself hours and hours of searching for things when it's actually time to use them.

FROM PAM:

Recently, we created a de-junking video to show people how to clean out their closets, cupboards, and drawers. In order to demonstrate how to de-junk a house, we had to have a messed-up set. The producer of the video was open to several possibilities. We could make the video on a real television set in a studio or do it in one of our homes. In any case, the set would have to be messed up so that we could show how to clean it up. We used my home.

As soon as I knew my house was going to be the place, I had about a month to scrape together enough rubbish to recreate my past. In just a few days, I had quite a nice collection of cereal boxes, Pepsi cans, milk cartons, newspapers, dog food cans, junk mail, and more. I accumulated the trash on one section of the kitchen counter, but within a week it started to scare me. It felt sickeningly familiar. I had to move the mess into the garage to save my sanity.

I put the word out to neighbors, friends, and family that I needed toys, stuffed animals, fabric, unfinished crafts, and any garage-sale–type junk. In a month, I had enough junk to successfully reenact my ugly past.

Since we wanted the video to show before and after scenes, it was decided that we would do the "after" shots the first day and the "before" shots the second day.

Two producers came from Los Angeles and a television crew from KATU-TV in Portland came the first day to videotape my kitchen, dining room, and every drawer and cupboard. Everything was perfect. The next day everyone returned to shoot the mess.

I had totally trashed the kitchen and dining room. The sinks were full of dishes and old food. (A week before the shoot, I had started growing some molds and saving left-over meals at room temperature.) The stovetop was caked with dried pancake batter and egg yoke. Every dish, glass, and cup was dirty, and there was no spot on the counters or any other horizontal surface without a pile at least six inches high. My husband, Terry, was dumbfounded. We got married long after my slob days, and he has come to enjoy our immaculate house.

It was actually quite fun to make the mess, especially because I knew that there was money in the budget for cleanup. Incidentally, it took three people six hours to make my house look the way it did before the shoot.

No one could believe I really lived that way, and they all accused me of exaggerating. (You'll have to see the video!) Peggy was the only one to back me up. That is, until my two older children came over.

Peggy Ann was the first one to come by. (Fifteen years ago, when I reformed, she was nine.) I couldn't wait to see her reaction. I introduced her to everyone, and they all stood waiting for her response.

She walked slowly through the devastation, taking in everything with a definite look of recollection. Then she spoke, "Well, it's ALMOST like it used to be." She paused, and I knew everyone was thinking that I did exaggerate, then she continued, "but you don't have any cat food on the kitchen floor!" It so happened that I did have cat food on the kitchen floor; she just hadn't seen it yet.

Then my son Michael dropped by (he was thirteen when I changed my ways). He walked into the mess with a confused but comforted look, as if he'd just found his favorite, old ratty teddy bear. He actually liked the mess and complimented me on its authenticity!

The making of this video was quite a mental adventure for me. I had just finished reading a fabulous book by Dr. Wayne Dyer, *You'll See It When You Believe It,* and I know his title is the truth. Jesus said, "It is done unto you as you believe." Back in 1977 when Peggy and I vowed we were going to get organized, we both BELIEVED we were going to do it. At that time our houses were both caves, but we were able to BELIEVE we were organized in spite of the way things looked. After six weeks of hard work, fueled by our new belief, we got to actually SEE what we had BELIEVED.

In the making of this video, I was able to see circumstances in my home that I knew were not the truth, just as Peggy and I had done 1977. It was all pretend and I knew it, and yet I had been in those same circumstances fifteen years before and the mess was NOT pretend. There is no difference. The messes were identical; it doesn't matter if one was make-believe or not. The person I was back in 1977, who believed she was organized, is no different from the person I am today, who knows I am organized. The results were identical, too. Both messes went away.

Start believing you are organized right now, in spite of how things look. Get that feeling that comes when you really believe something. Stop saying, "I'm so disorganized," or "I'm always late," or "I can't find anything." By announcing those kinds of statements, you only postpone the results you so dearly want.

REMEMBER, IT DOES NOT MATTER IF IT DOES NOT SHOW IMMEDIATELY ... IT WILL EVENTUALLY!

Seven

Gone With the Wind

During the fifteen years that we have been conducting workshops for the disorganized, we have noticed that about 75 percent of our clientele is overweight. That has never surprised us. Collectively, we have lost 104 pounds since becoming organized. When our homes were in a mess, our dining room tables were not only our craft centers but the place where we folded laundry and the drop off spot for everyone's miscellaneous incoming and outgoing junk.

By covering the one place where you are supposed to eat, a right-brainer will automatically expand his/her dining territory. It's our educated guess that you and your family eat over the sink (when you're worried about spills) and in every room of the house (when you're not).

If that's true, you have probably developed what we call free-range feeding, or "free-ranging." Our definition of free-ranging is: the taking in of any food (regardless of nutritional value), while standing, walking, driving, resting, working, bathing, talking on the telephone, or watching television.

FREE-RANGING IS VERY DANGEROUS! It can cause

accidents when a free-ranger drops food into his/her lap while trying to wrestle a Whopper and maneuver through traffic with one hand. FREE-RANGING IS VERY EXPENSIVE! An accident almost always causes an increase in insurance premiums. FREE-RANGING IS A NASTY HABIT. It is one of the causes of obesity, stains on furniture and carpeting, garbled telephone conversations, and sticky clickers to the TV. It'll stop a shopper at the door of most stores at the mall, with their rule of no food or drink beyond this point. In fact, all the litter on our highways and in our parks and waterways is caused by *careless* free-rangers.

If you make a rule that, from now on, you will eat only at your table, sitting down, we guarantee you'll lose weight, because your eating opportunities will be slashed in half. You'll also reduce the chance of hazards and cut down on the mess in your home, your car, and our beautiful country.

If you are a free-ranger, chances are you have free-range children. Television doesn't help. If you think about it, many of the food commercials show kids eating while they do just about everything. You see them hopscotching while eating a hot dog, skateboarding while munching cookies, and playing video games while drinking soda pop. The commercials give the impression that, unless you eat while you do other things, you are just not having much fun. The truth is, you miss a great deal of the pleasure of eating when you mix it with other activities.

If you are a hard-core free-ranger, you are probably doing a lot of unconscious eating. That means you don't even remember what you ate. Have you ever said something like, "I didn't have lunch today ... oh, except for the crackers and a little bit of peanut butter ... oh, and the doggy bag leftovers ... oh yeah, and the glass of grape juice and a chicken leg"? Often you can totally reconstruct several meals you've had when you thought you hadn't eaten a thing.

Here's a poem written about unconscious eating, by a former free-ranger.

DEAR JENNY CRAIG
by Pam Young

I made myself a sandwich
And something's really weird.
The crumbs are on the counter,
But the sandwich disappeared.

I can't believe I ate it
And I won't admit I did!
I know I ate a bite or two
While I was screwing on the lid
To the gallon jar of mayonnaise,
After licking off the knife
That was standing knee-deep in there
Treading mayo for its life.

I may have eaten just a half
Of that sandwich that I made.
I know I washed some down
With a glass of lemonade
That I poured to quench my awful thirst
After eating guacamole
Or maybe it was taco chips,
Or, no, the crescent roll. See
I smeared some peanut butter on the roll
And took a taste,
When my buds relayed the message
That unless I heaped, in haste,
A glob of homemade jelly
On the butter and the roll,
The overall experience
Would leave a gourmet hole.

So I carried out the order,
Drank some milk to wash it down
And when I put the carton back,
You won't believe it but I found
A Snickers Bar I'd started
And didn't have time to finish
So I'd hidden it with forethought
In a box of frozen spinach
Which I bought for just that reason,
'Cause my kids are little snackers.
I've learned from past experience,
They'll eat you out of crackers
And anything that's chocolate
And everything that's sweet.
They're worse than ants at picnics
When it comes to finding treats.

Which brings me back to wonder
If that's what happened to my sandwich.
Did my children spy my meal
And fail to understand which
Food is theirs and which is mine?
It's hard to keep things separate.
Those sneaky little snackers
Must have gotten awfully desperate.

OK, if I did consume it
And I must admit I'm stuffed;
Then where's that little voice I have
That says I've had enough?

I guess it's pretty obvious
By looking at my hips,
That more than fruits and vegetables
Have passed between my lips.

A small bite here, a swallow there,
Just how much I can't remember,
But according to my scale,
I've gained ten pounds since last September!

Free-ranging is for cows, and, if you think about it, look how big a heifer is! Could there be a correlation? Cows get to eat on the hoof, because they have FOUR stomachs to fill. You only have one. If you decide that from now on, you are going to fill yours only while seated at a table, you will be amazed at what a difference that simple change will make.

Getting Healthy

If you have ever had a New Year's resolution to lose weight and get in shape, and then by bathing suit season, you could kick yourself for the condition of your body, you are part of the majority. We think the main reason people fail at diets and physical fitness programs is that they are disorganized. To follow a diet plan and stay on a fitness routine, you have to be organized. By incorporating our plan into your card file, you will give yourself the direction you have lacked in your previous attempts. Before you read further, we want you to take ten minutes to make two short but very important lists. We'll tell you why, later.

The first list we want you to make is a list of reasons why you want to lose weight and get in condition. Just as we asked you, at the beginning of this book, to list some good reasons to get organized, we want you to figure out some good reasons to lose weight and get in shape. Here is a sample list to help you make yours.

WHY I WANT TO LOSE WEIGHT AND GET BACK IN SHAPE

My clothes hurt because they are so tight, but I refuse to move into the next size up.

I am not going to be a fat bride at my wedding or a fat mother at my children's weddings.

I don't like the looks I get from people who haven't seen me for a while. I think they are thinking, "Wow, what happened to her?"

My feet and knees are killing me because of the extra weight they're carrying.

I sense that my kids are embarrassed.

I'm embarrassed.

I feel left out of activities, because I don't have the energy to hike, ski, run, and play with my family like I used to.

My blood pressure is high, and I'm worried.

I have low self-esteem, because I don't like the way I look.

Once you have written down the negatives of being overweight and out of shape, next write down why you are not doing anything about this facet of your life. Here is a sample list.

WHY I HAVEN'T BEEN EATING RIGHT AND GETTING EXERCISE

I love chocolate, mayonnaise, chicken skin, beef, grease, butter, you name it. If it's fattening, I love it.

By avoiding exercise, I don't have to sweat and hurt afterward.

My schedule is already cramped. By not taking time to exercise, I have more time to do other things I enjoy.

By not exercising, I don't have to think about getting proper shoes and exercise equipment. I can spend the money on other things.

By eating the way I always do, I don't have to read up on what is healthy, and I don't have to buy a bunch of food that is foreign to me.

It's hot most of the time, and by not walking, I get to stay in my air-conditioned house.

It's always raining where I live, and by staying in my house, I don't have to go out and get cold, or buy waterproof attire so that I can walk in the rain.

When I am depressed or bored, if I eat, I feel better.

I love to eat in restaurants.

Now you have a list of reasons why you should lose weight and get in shape and a list of what has been keeping you from taking action. The two lists are very important, because they represent PAIN and PLEASURE. Besides being disorganized, two more reasons why you haven't been successful in this area are the ways you link PAIN and PLEASURE to eating and exercise.

We agree with many of the human behavioralists who claim we are motivated by PAIN and PLEASURE and that we will do far MORE to AVOID PAIN than we will to GET PLEASURE. For instance, if you love chocolate chip cookies, and someone hands you a warm, fresh Mrs. Field's chocolate chip cookie and says to you, "Here's a cookie, but don't eat it because you are on a diet," would you eat it? You would probably say, "Oh, big deal, I'll just eat this one." That's because, in that scenario, you have no pain linked with the eating of the cookie. At that moment, if you chose the cookie over the diet, where would the pain be? It wouldn't be there.

Now let's say the cookie-giver hands you a fresh, hot-out-of-the-oven Mrs. Field's chocolate chip cookie and says, "Here's a cookie, but don't eat it because it is laced with arsenic." You wouldn't eat it because arsenic poisoning would be very painful. In staying on a healthy eating program, you will be faced with temptations all the time. Unless you can associate more pain than pleasure with eating all of the temptations you'll face, you'll eat them.

Until you associate enough pain with being overweight, you will not eliminate the problem. In fact, until you can associate enough pain with being overweight, you will continue to GAIN. If you are overweight now and you are not going to do anything about it, YOU ARE GOING TO GAIN MORE. That first list of reasons to lose the weight is automatically a list of the negatives in your life, caused by the extra weight. Unless it produces enough pain for you to want to take action, you won't.

If scientists say that we will do more to avoid pain than we will to seek pleasure, it's a wonder everyone doesn't have at least fifty pounds to lose. As far as exercise is concerned, getting into shape hurts. If something hurts, it's our nature to avoid it. As far as food is concerned, eating is pleasurable. There is no pain involved with eating, unless your jaw is out of kilter, you have a sore throat, or you have tooth problems. The pain of eating fattening foods comes three weeks after you ate the food and you can't zip up your pants. What you need to do is turn up the pain when it comes to eating and turn down the pain when it comes to exercise.

Turning Up the Pain When It's Time to Eat

Since it's our nature to enjoy food, the best way to turn up the pain factor is to associate pain with eating fattening foods. What if that same cookie-giver said, "Would you like a cookie?" and you responded by using your "air horn"? What if you promised yourself that, for the next week, whenever you're faced with unexpected temptations, you'll use your own personal, inner air horn?

Years ago, we read a book on dieting, in which the author told about his strategy to turn up the pain. He needed to lose a lot of weight, and he had failed in the past. He knew himself well enough that he put into his weight-loss plan enough pain that if he didn't succeed, he would be sick. He was Jewish and had lost many family members in the Holocaust. He had his attorney draw up a legal and binding promissory note, stating that if he did not lose the weight he wanted to lose in one year from the date he started his diet, the American Nazi Party would receive five thousand dollars. The thought of that hideous group receiving all that money kept him true to his personal promise to lose the weight.

You probably don't need to take such drastic measures, but you are the only one who really knows yourself. If you decide you really need to muscle yourself, perhaps you could pick an organization you absolutely abhor and promise them your first-born if you don't reach your weight goal. (Be careful with that suggestion; you may have days when you'd be tempted to gorge yourself.) For us, it took posting that first list we asked you to make (the reasons why you want to lose weight and get in shape) on our refrigerators and keeping it in our purses so that, when we went grocery shopping, we stayed on track. Healthy eating starts in your mind and can take a detour at the grocery store, if you are not prepared.

Turning Down the Pleasure When It's Time to Eat

We do not want you to make eating less pleasurable, but you will be changing your tastes so that nourishing foods are more pleasing and fattening foods are less pleasing. One of the wonderful things about humans is that our pleasures can change. You can truly learn to enjoy foods that are good for you. We live in a time when there are so many new foods that are fat- and sugar-free and taste very good. Once you get used to these foods, going back to the fattening fare is awful. A good example is milk. We were raised on whole milk. By the time our kids were born, we were drinking 2 percent. Now we drink skim milk. To go back to whole milk would be like drinking a glass of whipping cream. Soda pop is another example. Drinking regular pop when, for the last fifteen years, we've been drinking diet soda, would be like drinking liquid cotton candy. Since the change to new and different foods is relatively painful (no one likes change), that's when you need the first list foremost in your thoughts.

Turning Up the Pleasure When It's Time to Exercise

From our own experience, when it comes to working out, if we don't enjoy the type of exercise we do, we will end up on the couch watching reruns of Jack La Lanne. You must pick forms of exercise that will fit your personality. Walking, biking, horseback riding, ice skating, mountain climbing, skiing, dancing, step aerobics, football, golf, swimming, whatever sounds fun. Remember, your basic nature is fun-loving. If you try to take on a grueling aerobic program like Ordell maintains, you'll peter out on about the second set of one-arm push-ups.

Once you pick out some forms of exercise that sound fun, get the proper attire and equipment. There's nothing worse than using your daughter's "Little Tike" if you want to bicycle. The best way to kill the joy of a sport is to have the wrong equipment. Skis that are too long will send you to the lodge on a stretcher, way before the rest of the group is ready to quit. A bowling ball with holes spread too far to match your reach will keep you from being invited into the ladies' league. Golfing with your husband's clubs will slow up the game and cause a tie-up of aggravated players behind you. If you are borrowing your daughter's bike, your sister's skis, your brother's ball, or your husband's clubs, you're telling yourself one thing—THIS ACTIVITY IS TEMPORARY. Make it a priority to have the right equipment and apparel, and make it belong to YOU. You'll have a much better chance at staying with whatever you choose.

Don't Forget About Schmidky

Remember that Schmidky is your pleasure seeker. Schmidky already knows everything that you love to do and everything that you love to eat. Have a meeting with him and tell him you need to change some of your likes and dislikes. Tell him you are going to cut your intake of fat to twenty grams a day, which will make you happy. Tell him you are going to start an exercise program that will be fun. Tell him that, because of your new decisions, you are going to be healthier and live longer, that you are going to look good in your clothes, feel good about yourself, climb stairs and not get out of breath, move with grace and ease, be able to ski, run, hike, and play with your family and feel better, because you will be eating foods that are healthy. He'll start to work immediately to make sure that your orders are carried out.

Eating the Cards

Richard Simmons created what he calls Deal-a-Meal. He took a healthy diet and put the food on cards. On any given day, the eater uses the cards to direct what he/she will eat for the day. We were surprised when Simmons came on TV with his new program, because we were eating cards long before he was. In our weight-loss program we call "Gone with the Wind," we used the Weight Watchers diet and transferred the various foods onto cards. Then we incorporated them into our rotating card file system. For instance, in the Weight Watchers program, it is suggested that you drink eight glasses of water every day. We wrote the word "water" on eight blue 3 × 5 pieces of construction paper. Each day, as we drank a glass of water, we'd move one of the water cards to the next day. We used other colored cards to represent fats, protein, milk, fruits, vegetables, etc. If we'd eaten all our cards, we'd have to go to bed.

You can use the card plan for any healthy diet. The American Heart Association diet is very good, or you could use a diet your doctor recommends. List each food and the amount you can have daily (in the case of foods like red meat, eggs, and cheese, list the amount you can have weekly) and transfer the list to cards. The cards can go into your card file along with all of your other cards. It's that easy!

Exercise

Many physical fitness experts agree that, three times a week for twenty minutes, we should do aerobic exercise to raise our heart rate. In Chapter 4, we had you make out an exercise card to direct you to work out three times a week. It is important to check with your doctor before starting any physical fitness routine, but as soon as you do that, JUST DO IT!

So, there are five ways for you to be successful at losing weight and getting in shape.

1. Make your table functional by clearing it off and using it for dining.

2. Put a moratorium on free-ranging.
3. Link pain to eating the wrong foods and pleasure to exercising.
4. Find a nutritional diet plan, put it on 3 × 5 cards, and incorporate it into your card file.
5. Use the exercise card you made in Chapter 4.

If you can do those five things, you are going to be healthy and happy. Remember, though, you didn't get out of shape in a week, and you're not going to get back into shape in a week. Also, one of your traits is a childlike nature, so be gentle with yourself or you'll rebel.

Eight

The Inside Story

After all of our efforts to get organized and have clean houses, we gradually began to realize that something was wrong. True, the janitorial duties were being handled according to plan, but we hadn't yet learned how to deal with our families' tide of unconscious clutter. In the bigger picture, it doesn't matter that the oven is cleaned on a regular basis if the kitchen is cluttered with backpacks, schoolbooks, home improvement tools, junk mail, and the personal belongings of various family members. If the room is messy, it leaves a dirty impression. Regardless of the cleanliness on the inside, the outward appearance caused by a careless clan can give a clean home mistaken identity.

One of the main problems of staying organized is the challenge of getting the other members of the family to be accountable for their own tracks.

We had been receiving hundreds of letters from homemakers, pleading with us to tell them how to get family members to cooperate. With so many requests to solve that problem and our own inability to clear up our situations, we knew we had to find the answers. It took us over a year and what we learned is in Chapter 11.

Before we tell you our solutions, we want to share with you the dirty story that led up to finding them. We have to take you back in time to March 24, 1987. Hazel Dell, Washington, (a sleepy community established in a hazelnut orchard, three miles north of Vancouver), inside the home of Peggy Jones.

Six A.M. I woke up to the cheerful voices of my sister and her walking friends, as they marched past my house on their daily four-mile hike. I rolled over and looked at my mate. Danny's mouth was slightly open as he snored softly, his morning breath gently puffing into my face every six seconds. Not ready to stir, I adjusted my breathing so that our exhales matched. I stood it as long as I could.

"Time to get up, Danny," I said.

"Huh?"

"Time to get up. The walkers just went by. It's six."

"Okay ..."

"Danny, do you think we should start walking?"

"Where?" He yawned and stretched at the same time.

"With Pam's group. It sounds like they have a lot of fun. Look at us. We're still in bed. Don't you feel guilty, lying here? By the time we get up, they've done their exercise for the day. What do we do? We sleep as late as we possibly can.

"I worry about us now that we're forty. You know how high your cholesterol was two years ago ... well, I'll bet it's gone up. I'm going to make an appointment for you to get it checked. Pam says we should be drinking more water, too. At Weight Watchers, they told her everybody needs to drink at least eight glasses a day. We need to do that ... so what do you think?"

"Yeah, I'll have a glass of water."

"No, I mean, what do you think about walking? Danny? ... Danny! Danny, do you think we should start walking?" There was no answer from him, so I answered myself, "Yeah, maybe in the summer, when it warms up."

The morning started out the same as any other busy weekday. Five people, all getting ready to leave the house at the same time, caused the usual circus. The bathrooms were taken by the two teenagers, and the kitchen showed signs of a hurried breakfast, but this morning was unusually tense. I had been out of town for a couple of days, to tape some television spots with my sister, and the family was feeling the effects of my absence.

"Babe, are we out of shampoo?" Danny called to me from the shower.

"Just a minute!" I dashed to the supply cupboard in the hall. I was used to shopping in bulk at Cramco (it was really called Costco, but we renamed it because we could never cram all we bought into the car), so I was sure I would find an extra gallon of shampoo. I rummaged through the surplus inventory of products. I found three economy-size cans of industrial-strength bathroom cleaner, two gallons of Windex, a tub of Epsom Salts, six Comet cleansers (in institutional-size cans), a pound of Q-tips, a pound of Band-Aids, a quart of Liquid Woolite, two aerosol cans of hair spray (for professional use only), and a half gallon of Scope. There was no shampoo.

I flew to my suitcase, thinking there might be some hotel shampoo in there, left over from my trip. I pawed through the clothes and found nothing but an empty plastic travel container I'd used for conditioner.

"Peggy! Are you getting the shampoo or what? I'm running out of hot water!" Danny's voice was urgent.

As was often the case throughout my life, my right brain coughed up the solution. I ran back to the supply cupboard, grabbed the Liquid Woolite, and filled the little plastic bottle.

"Here you go, Babe. Use this. I guess it's time for me to make a run over to Cramco again."

I was making the bed when Danny came in with a towel wrapped around him. "Boy, does that shampoo ever suds up! I had trouble rinsing it out."

"Hmm ..." I didn't look at him. I went on making the bed. "How come you never make the bed, Danny?"

"Cause you do."

"If I didn't make it, would you?

"I don't know. Probably not. What do I have to wear, Babe?"

"I don't know. I've been gone. Did you get your clothes from the cleaners?"

"I wasn't aware you'd taken them in."

"I took them before I left."

"Well, that doesn't do me a lot of good right now, does it?" His face glared down into mine.

I was just about to say, "Now wait just a minute, pal. Who made me your slave?" when Danny pivoted to go to his closet and fell into my open suitcase. "Did you have any plans to unpack this thing, or were you just going to leave it out here on the rug?" He wouldn't accept help getting out of the luggage, and waved me out of his way. "I'm gonna be late for work. Just see if you can put an outfit together for me, would you?"

He hurried to the bathroom, and I heard the hair dryer go on. I looked in his closet and scrounged up an exhausted ensemble. It was obvious he needed new clothes. That wasn't my fault, I reassured myself. After all, he had been a uniformed policeman for the last couple of years, and his new job in Investigations had recently put him in plain clothes. Unfortunately, his wardrobe was skimpy and outdated. His aversion to fitting rooms and tailors had kept him away from the mall.

"Peggy!" Danny yelled from the bathroom. "Can you catch the back of my hair? I can't get it to stay down."

I rushed in to help him. He looked like one of the Three Stooges. Who would think that hair and wool wouldn't be the same? I took the brush from Danny and made a futile attempt to calm the coif.

"I think you blew it dry wrong. I'm afraid it doesn't want to go down."

Danny grabbed the professional hair spray and gave his head a good going-over. Then he took the brush and tried to force the follicles into place. They stuck together in wet clumps. I put the hand mirror back in the drawer.

"How does it look in the back?" It looked worse than I had ever seen it look in twenty years. "Fine," I said, hoping he'd take my word for it. After all, what were his options ... wash it over again and this time use Joy or Four Paws Magic Coat (flea and tick shampoo), wear a hat, or call in sick? There were no other options.

Danny stormed back into the bedroom. I shoved the suitcase under the bed, out of his way. He threw on the stupid outfit I had laid out for him. The slacks were about an inch too short (shrunken victims of too many tumbles in the Maytag), but he was moving so fast, it was hard to notice. I followed him as he started to leave. "See you tonight." He dutifully kissed me, a quick, off-centered smack, and started through the front door.

Our two German shepherds had been on one of their all-night digs, and there was a huge pile of dirt from the planter on the first step of the porch. Danny's long, rubberlike legs absorbed the surprise of running up and over the mound of dirt, and he recovered gracefully as he negotiated the hill like a flamingo.

"I'll get this cleaned up, Danny. You go on to work.... Don't forget to drink your water."

"My water?"

"Your water. Remember, Sissy says you're supposed to drink eight glasses every day?"

He muttered something I didn't care to ask him to repeat, and he was off to fight crime.

I went back into the house, making a mental note to get a shovel as soon as the kids left for school.

"Did you make my lunch, Mom?" Chris, my fifteen-year-old, asked. He was pouring himself a glass of apple juice.

"No. Get a dollar out of the money drawer."

"There's nothing in there," Jeff, fourteen, said. "I already looked."

"Where's my purse?!"

We started hunting. "Look under those newspapers, or maybe it's under that pile of clean clothes. Somebody go look in the car.

"Whose cereal bowl is this? Allyson, is this your bowl?"

"No, I didn't get any cereal. All the boxes in the pantry are empty."

"What!? Who keeps doing that? Don't put the box back in the cupboard if it's empty. How many times do I have to tell you guys, you don't put empty boxes back in the pantry? If the box is empty, put it in the trash!"

"Mom, will you tell Chris to quit hogging all the hot water? He was in the shower for fifteen minutes!"

"I was not."

"Were too."

"Was not."

"Knock it off, you guys!"

"Here's your purse, Mom. I found it in the car." Ally tossed it on the counter and started to leave.

"Oh, good. Here, Chris, here's a five. You and Jeff stick together at lunch and bring me back my change. Put the jug of apple juice back, Chris. Ally, come and get your lunch money. Jeff, clean up your mess in the bathroom before you leave."

"Mom, can you go on a field trip with my class next Wednesday? My teacher says the snakes aren't out yet." Ally was waving a permission slip at me.

"Snakes! Where are you going?!"

"To the Ridgefield Wildlife Refuge."

"Oh, no, Ally, I can't do that! The teacher promised me there wouldn't be any snakes the year I went with Jeff's class, and they were everywhere! I had to be carried back to the bus. It was humiliating! I'm surprised Miss McKinney would even ask!"

"Mom, there's swimming after school and I have to work tonight. Can you wash my uniform? It's on the floor in my closet."

"I'll try. You'd better bring it upstairs and put it in the hall so I don't forget. Bring up your other laundry, too. You guys need to do that every morning so I know how much there is to do. Come on, you guys, you're going to miss the bus."

When the last one had gone out the door, I slumped down onto the couch. My life was not running smoothly.

I knew what I wanted it to be like. I wanted a modern-day Walton's Mountain, only with more money, a housekeeper, and no in-laws living with me.

The children would adore each other, and honor and respect their father and me. They'd be so used to helping that I could say, "Go do your chores," and they'd know exactly what I meant by that. Our home would be clean, cozy, and filled with laughter, and we'd all look forward to worshiping together on Sundays.

Each morning I'd go to my warm, sunny kitchen and make the coffee. The children would make their own breakfast, and, one by one, they'd rinse their dishes and cheerfully put them in the dishwasher. The sink and counters would be spotless, inviting me to start preparing a few things for dinner.

The pace would be unhurried, but steady, as each one would shower and dress (in outfits set out the night before). They'd make their beds, sort their laundry, and get ready to leave for school.

As the last one stepped happily onto the school bus, Danny and I would linger over a tender good-bye kiss at the front door. Then I would enjoy a second cup of coffee in my peaceful, lovely living room, as I curled up with a good book. At the end of a chapter or two, I would check the soup in my crockpot and jump into a nice, hot shower.

I would put on a size-five pair of name-dropping jeans and a crisp, white cotton blouse, step into a sporty pair of tennis shoes, put on coordinating earrings, fix my hair and do my makeup, and, with an hour to kill before work, I'd check the 3 × 5 housekeeping cards in my card file kit. I'd set aside jobs for the housekeeper and do a bit of light housework myself. With soft music in the background, I'd rinse out a few hand-washables, shine the glass-top coffee table, set out the china for dinner, and freshen the guest room.

Then my sister would come over to work on our novel.

"MMMM ... it sure smells good in here," she'd say.

"Really? It's probably the stuffing I made for the Cornish game hens, or maybe it's the soup simmering."

"Well, it smells wonderful!"

We'd work until noon, do lunch at the Alexis, drop by our office to get our mail, and knock off at three.

I would return to my home-sweet-home, and the aroma of a delicious dinner would melt away any stress I'd collected. My happy honor-rollers would come home from school, and over a nice, tall glass of iced tea, they'd share their day with me.

Danny would call to see if he could run any errands for me on his way home from work. The children would ask what they could do to help with dinner.

At five P.M., my husband would spring through the door and hand me a small bouquet of wild violets he'd picked. He'd put his arms around me and say, "These reminded me of you. You're so delicate that a good wind would blow you away!" Then we'd sit out on the deck in matching chaise longues, and, while sipping a fragrant glass of lemonade, we'd tell each other about our fabulous day. We would enjoy our meal together as a family, and afterward, each one would rinse his or her own dishes and put them in the dishwasher, and the last one would start it up. Then Danny would insist that I relax and read the paper, while he and the children scoured the pots and pans, polished the sinks and wiped the counters, damp-mopped the kitchen floor, and emptied the garbage.

Unfortunately, Walton's Mountain was only a fantasy. The only mountain close to my house was Mount St. Helen's!

MEANWHILE ... Salmon Creek, Washington (a sleepier community about three miles north of Hazel Dell), outside the home of Pam Young.

MARCH 24, 1987:

I got back from my sunrise trudge with a heavy heart to match my thighs. My friend, Carole, and I had started walking after weighing up the Christmas pounds we put on. To date, we figured we had walked about 320 miles, and we still hadn't lost a gram. Carole had even gained a pound more than what she had weighed the night she waddled into a Weight Watchers meeting, threw herself onto the stage, and cried, "HELP ME!" She had even resorted to wearing what she termed her Watergate wardrobe. She said it consisted of several full-cut garments that covered up everything.

I had started to gradually disappear into a cushion of cellulite when I stopped dating a midlife jogger. It had been a relief to slow down from the fast lane at the athletic club. Now I was blessed with a man who had a rowing machine stored in his attic, and whose idea of exercise was bringing it down for his annual garage sale and hauling it back up afterward.

Back in January, when I had bumped into Carole in the grocery store (we were both reaching for the same pork roast), it had been like running into myself in the mirror. We were the same age, height, and weight, and we had identically proportioned bodies.

"Carole, how are you? I haven't seen you since ..."

"Since that time we had lunch and ended up going out to dinner after that."

"Gad, how long ago was that?"

As we blocked the aisle, catching up on each other's activities, there was silent recognition that we had each put on a little weight. (We confided, later, that we had both felt a rush of "grocery-cart guilt" until we realized that our purchases had been similar in their fat content.)

"Oh, Carole, I've gained ten pounds since Thanksgiving! I've just got to get a hold of myself! The trouble with me is that I'm self-indulgent. That's all there is to it. Look at the calories in this cart! I mean, please, I know I shouldn't have real butter and mayonnaise and those cookies ... I don't even remember putting them in there."

"Hey, self-indulgence is my middle name. I'll be at home all alone, minding my own business, and I'll think ... *Hmmm, what sounds good?* and before I know it, I've answered myself ... *Well, how 'bout some ice cream?* ... and then I think, *You don't want it blank! Let's put some chopped cashews, a little chocolate syrup, and Cool Whip on top!* There's a little Mr. Sweet Tooth inside of me, and he's a real hog!"

"What are we going to do?"

"Well, I started walking last week. I go four miles a day with Ann and Claudia. You oughta come along."

I joined the walkers, but here I was, three months and 320 miles later, still heavy. My only solace was that if I HADN'T exercised, I'd probably weigh ten pounds more than I did now.

As I reached my house, it didn't help my cloudy spirit to see the contents of my garbage can strewn all over the driveway. My front yard looked like a landfill. I was embarrassed, especially since I had written three books on getting organized, and I knew that this mess would delight Mrs. Dorchester, the neighborhood jogging gossip. Her network of rumor mongers always enjoyed finding any evidence to show that I needed to take some of my own advice.

As I picked up the junk in the yard, I thought about what had happened to me since Peggy and I had become organized twelve years earlier. We'd traveled all over the country helping homemakers improve their domestic affairs. Things had definitely improved for me too, but they were far from perfect. I was still plagued, and probably always would be, with the effects of my genetic disorder.

The garbage was a good example. The lid on the can had been squashed flat in the winter of '82 (it was buried under the snow when I ran over it with the car), but instead of buying a whole new can, I always balanced the useless lid on top of its overstuffed contents. Consequently, every garbage day there was a race to see who would get to my refuse first, Vancouver Sanitary Service or the neighbors' dog, Lasagna (a garbage and Labrador retriever mix).

In recent years, I'd had some drastic changes occur in my life (two of my children had gone away to college). Now, even more distressing, they both had returned home for spring break! Joanna, fourteen, my born-organized child, and I had become quite comfortable without the chaos that her two siblings could generate. When they returned, the house submerged under the clutter before I realized what had happened. With the yard cleaned up, I vowed to get a new garbage can lid (I wondered if I could buy the top without the bottom), and I went into the house.

As I opened the door, Chelsea Marie, my basset hound puppy, greeted me with what had been one of my good high heels. I lobbed it in the vicinity of her toy box, which was filled with an assortment of objects she had, out of boredom, confiscated and destroyed. It contained a colorful variety of leather shoe casualties, a fuzzy assortment of the children's prized stuffed animals that they had collected over the years, and a potpourri of things we'd neglected to put away. The mark of a teething puppy was everywhere.

Walking into the living room, I remembered there were four extra bodies staying over. Fraternity brothers of Mike's, my oldest offspring, were conked out in their clothes on the living room floor like a gathering of park-bench bums. Their party remains were everywhere. A rented movie was still in the VCR, and I cringed at the titles of the other two on top of the TV. I didn't care to know the name of the one they had fallen asleep to. I reminded myself that they were all over twenty-one.

The morning-after kitchen was testimony to a great night before. The refrigerator was stripped of everything edible, including some borderline potato salad and a bowl of leftover beans that no one had liked in the first place. The home-moviegoers had obviously enjoyed my absentee hospitality. (I had gone out to dinner and to a movie, then had slipped to bed while the Delta Upsiloners were engrossed in their video rentals.) Since it was only 8:15, I decided to let them sleep, while I took a shower and started polishing my half of an article Peggy and I had to finish for *McCall's* magazine.

On the way to my desk in the corner of the living room, I tripped on the arm of one of the sleepers. He didn't move. *If the children's father still lived here, God forbid, these people would not be sacked out in my living room like this. We would have come home last night and he would have clicked off the TV and thrown a huge fit over the mess.*

I could feel my body start to tense, thinking of the scene that would have occurred. I knew from experience that I hated confrontations like that. Still, I knew that as soon as these vacationing scholars stirred, I would have to tell them how upset I was with the way my living room and kitchen looked. I knew it would be a hassle to get them to clean everything up. Since I hate situations where I have to be the "bad guy," I didn't relish the inevitable clash.

I wish there was a man I could hire to come over and throw a fit for me. I would leave for an hour, and, when I came back, everything would be straightened out. I'd find his ad in the yellow pages: "ATTENTION, SINGLE MOMS: Sgt. Stickler will take care of all disciplinary actions in your home. I will put an end to unnecessary bickering, enforce punishments, make rules, and deliver lectures approved by the mother. Hourly rate or salary. Call 574-MEAN, and I'll wear the pants in your family!"

I looked at the rough draft of the article we were writing. The title made me squirm, "Fifteen Hassle-free Ways to Get Your Family to Help Around the House." It implied manipulation, and I didn't like the idea of GETTING anybody to help around the house; I wanted them to WANT to do their part. Besides, the fact that our article was going to be published in a women's magazine implied that it would be the woman who would be doing the manipulation; the mother would still be responsible for domestic order. *Sports Illustrated* would never think of featuring an article with that title. Why? Because most men don't feel that the house is their responsibility, and they would never read it.

I glanced back at the living room. *How can I possibly contribute to this article when my house looks like a mission house on skid row? I'd do better writing about the hazards of being a single parent. At least I'd be writing about what I know! The 15 million women like me would probably love to read about somebody else who has had to raise her children by herself.*

I had assumed full responsibility for my three kids when they were four, nine, and twelve. Their father had moved away after the divorce, and I was left to raise them without the power that comes when two parents stand together against the constant challenge of growing children. So many times I had wished that I could say, "You'll have to ask your dad," or "Wait until your father gets home." Instead, I was the only one there to help them through the tangle of thoughts and feelings of growing up.

As a single mother, I went to PTA meetings alone. I was their only parent who rooted for them when they participated in their sports activities, praised them when they succeeded, consoled them when they were upset, and disciplined them when they did something wrong. That was the hard part. It isn't fun to have to make unpopular decisions.

I remember the time when Peggy Ann was furious with me for grounding her for a month. "We'll never be friends!" she cried (as only a teenage soap opera fanatic can). I wanted to be lenient and cut the grounding period in half, but I stiffened and replied, "I have plenty of friends, and I don't need you for a friend! YOU are my daughter!" She was livid, then cool throughout the sentence. (Today we are best friends.)

I glanced down at Mike as he slept. Except for the mustache, he looked just like he did when he was a child. As I watched him sleep, I felt so thankful that I had been able to be home with all my children as they grew up. I had never agreed with the idea that it was "quality time" that was important when raising children. I think it's quantity time that counts. A child can't be expected to concentrate all the important things he or she feels and thinks into some arbitrary hour or day that a parent designates as "quality time."

When Mike was two, he had interrupted my house-cleaning seventeen times in one hour! I'd counted them because I wanted to be able to justify to my husband why I could never get the whole house cleaned up. One of his interruptions was just to show me the inside of the dog's lips; unimportant by my standards, but a great discovery in his life.

In the end, the person who is there all the time is the one who gives quality time. I was glad that I hadn't missed any part of my children's lives. They had grown up so fast! I had such wonderful times with them, but there had been some hard times, too.

It's difficult bringing up children when two parents are actively involved. When one parent has the whole responsibility, it can be overwhelming. On one of our visits to the TV show "The 700 Club," my sister and I talked to the talent coordinator, Jackie Mitchum, who had reared a son by herself. She told us that there were times when she felt overburdened by the responsibility. During an exceptionally stressful time, she cried out, "Lord! I cannot be father and mother to this child." The Lord spoke to her heart and said, "I didn't call you to be the father and mother to this child, I called you to be his mother. I will be his father." From that point on, she said everything was much easier. Her son is now a very successful pastor.

I had always known that I wasn't alone when the kids were growing up. Whenever I was confused about what to do, or swallowed up by some problem, I knew that God was with me. That power has far more influence than the presence of any biological father.

I knew I could write volumes on my experiences as a single parent, but right now I needed to work on the article.

At 11:30 the guys started to come to life. The instant that the sleep was out of their eyes, I started on them to get the place cleaned up. I began with what I would describe as mild scolding, which promptly turned into moderate complaining. By the time I left to meet my sister for lunch, I was repulsed by the sound of my own voice, but at least my house looked like the kind of place where the author of a book on home organization just might live.

As Peggy and I stood in line at the Ron Det Vous (one of Hazel Dell's finest restaurants), we were both out of whack and preoccupied with our domestic state of affairs. Normally we would both be in whack, so the mood in the air was gloomy.

"You're awful quiet."

"Awfully quiet."

"Well, *pardone*, grammar queen!"

"Oh, I'm sorry. I'm just tired, I guess. I think I've got jet lag."

"Sissy?"

"Yeah?"

"We stayed on the West Coast. I think you only get to lag when you change time zones."

"Well, then I've got trip lag, and I didn't sleep very well either. I had a bank statement dream."

"A bank statement dream?"

"Yeah, I kept trying to find the mistake, but I never did. I spent the whole night looking for missing checks and deposit receipts. When I woke up, I needed a nap."

"When I go out of town, everything falls apart, and it takes me two or three days to get things back under control. Stuff really piles up fast. You can't see the top of my dresser for all the mail and Danny's junk on it ... and the laundry! While I was gone nobody did a thing ... No, I take that back. Danny had each of the kids wash and dry a load, but do you think they folded any of it? Of course not! It's all in a pile on the couch. It's like they think some laundry fairy will come through in the night, fold their clothes, and put them neatly back in their drawers! They don't even bring their laundry to where I sort it. I get so sick of having to drag everybody's dirty clothes from their rooms to the washer. I've lost my feist."

"Why do you do it?"

"Because if I didn't, it wouldn't get done."

"That's disgusting!"

"I know it is! And you know what else? This morning, Danny had the NERVE to criticize my sorting procedure!"

"Huh?"

"Yeah. He said I shouldn't put the dirty laundry in piles in the hall. That's where I have to sort the clothes."

"Well, it'd be a little hard to do it in a laundry room with a batch of eleven German shepherd puppies in there."

"Nine. Rosie's *first* litter was eleven."

"Oh."

"Where was I?"

"Dirty laundry—piles in the hall ..."

"Oh, yeah. Danny's no laundry expert! He wouldn't need ANY place to make piles, because he doesn't know you have to separate the colors! He'd throw 'em all in together, like the time I had the flu and he washed the pink throw rug with his black Dockers and underwear. He even threw in his tie!"

Finally it was our turn at the cash register, where Ron's wife took our order. We got a booth and waited for the hot pastramis to come to us.

"Sissy, do you think people who read our books picture our houses just immaculate?"

"Sure, they do."

"That makes me feel bad."

"It shouldn't. We've never claimed to be perfect. We've always admitted that we have a problem with organization. Besides, we were gone for three days. Why should we feel guilty for getting behind on the house, when we weren't even there?

"I hate the pressure of everything in the house falling on the woman's shoulders. Give me a break! It's not women's work inside and men's work outside! It's people-who-live-in-the-house work!"

"That's true, but a lot has to change in the male brain before it'll show up in the laundry room. Remember when we were at the vet and Dr. Slocum asked if we were working on a new project?"

"Yeah. I told him we were putting together a class to get

husbands to do half, and he said, 'Half of what?' When you said, 'Half of the household management, cooking, and child care,' he looked at you like you'd told him he needed to gupvail and fleckhammer his vendecrod more often. Your words did not compute."

"Yeah, but I'll bet those words would draw a blank with most men. Course there is that ... what's his name ... that preacher on television ... he does everything!"

"I wish there was a way to keep the house under control without nagging. I get so frustrated with everybody. When five people each leave out a few things, the place looks a mess even if it's clean. I mean, who cares if the blinds are dusted and light fixtures shine, when there's junk everywhere you look?"

"I'm just as guilty as the next guy. I left my makeup and curlers all over the bathroom counter, and I haven't even unpacked yet! But I feel like I'm responsible for everybody else, too, and that's not fair.

"You should see the house right now! It's a cave because, ever since I got home, my energy's been on the *McCall's* article. I haven't had time to do the breakfast dishes, so the kitchen's a mess; there's a huge pile of laundry to fold; we're out of groceries, and everybody's finger is pointed at me!"

"Well, I left my house clean, but everybody's MAD at me. Last night, before I went out with Terry, I threw a fit over Peggy's messes everywhere and she finally cleaned them up, but then Mike and his friends came over and made new ones. All I do is nag. I'm sick of the sound of my own voice."

We ate our lunch and talked about how we'd like things to be different.

"You know what I'd like? I'd like it if everybody just automatically cleaned up after himself, that's all! If they'd just take care of their own messes. Doesn't that make sense? If you trim your beard over the sink, clean up the whiskers before you leave the bathroom."

"Yeah, and if you take a bath, you clean the ring."

"And the last guy out of the bed makes it."

"Right! How about when you use the last square of toilet paper, you replace the roll?"

"Absolutely! Who buys the toilet paper?"

"The one with the most time, but the guy who shops doesn't have to haul the stuff from the car or put it away."

"That's fair. Who cooks?"

"I love to cook. But I shouldn't have to do the dishes."

"Of course not! Each eater should do his own dishes!"

"What about the pots and pans?"

"You don't touch them! If you cook the meal, they clean up after it!"

"Whoa, that would be interesting."

"What do you mean?"

"Think about it ... they're used to being served and cleaned up after. They wouldn't like that."

"Well, it's only fair."

"I know that, but just because it's fair doesn't mean they'd like it. How would you like it if, all of a sudden, we came here and ate our lunch and then found out we had to bus our own dishes and help out in the kitchen before we could leave? You'd hate it! Ron would be out of business in less than a week!"

"I see what you mean. But here, we're paying for the service. At home it's all free."

"That makes me wild. My time is not free!"

"Maybe you should start charging for meals and kitchen work."

"Yeah, or maybe I oughta go on a strike like that lady in *People* magazine did."

"What ever happened to her?"

"I don't know. Nothing, I guess."

"When I remarry, you can bet my husband will take care of himself! I won't be waiting on him hand and foot! He'll have to get up out of that recliner chair and do his half."

"Yeah, but he'll be used to it. He'll know what it takes to run a home because he's been on his own. Danny was twenty when we got married. He went from being taken care of by his mother to being waited on by me."

"You were a fool to get that started."

"Yeah, but I thought it was fun for a while ... and then we had the three kids all in three years 'cause you told me you can't get pregnant if you're nursing, and we got a bigger house and German shepherds and a cockatiel and three cats and I started a business.... I don't know when, exactly, but waiting on everybody and picking up after them stopped being fun."

"What are you going to do?"

"I'm going to go home and throw a fit! I'll line the kids up, and, through clenched teeth, I'll demand that they take an interest in having a clean house! I'll look Danny in the eye and tell him exactly what's wrong, and I'll insist things change! I'll tell him the days of "Father Knows Best" are over!"

"Schwooo ... I love it!"

"I'll say, 'Look, Danny, while you're propped up in your easy chair reading the evening paper, I'm sweating over a hot stove!'"

"Oh, that's good."

"Yeah. I'll say, 'You expect me to wash your clothes and have them hanging in your closet, all starched and ironed, and what thanks do I get? ... none!'"

"Yeah!"

"I'll say, 'Who balances the checkbook? Who picks up the boys from swimming practice and tennis classes? Who takes Ally to horseback riding lessons, and who takes the dogs to get their shots? Me! I mean, I!'"

"Ooo, yeah, watch your grammar."

"Yeah, I don't want him correcting me on anything! I'll say, 'Danny, the time has come for you to bond with the dogs!'"

"What'll he say?"

"He's a reasonable man. He'll see that things have to change. He's always real open and receptive to whatever I need. I'll just sit down with him and explain how I feel, and everything'll be fine."

We finished our lunch and, grateful to stand up and distribute the weight of the pastrami, went to our office to proofread the article. Our fifteen "hassle-free" ideas were merely Band-Aid tips that would cover up the real problem ... lack of willing cooperation. We wished there were some way to cause the whole family to become aware and accountable for their share of the load, because we were trying to do it ALL, and we were being swamped by the backwash of people, places, and things.

Nine

Can This Marriage Be Saved?

I went back to my cave after Pam and I sent the article. I felt as if I needed a nap, partly because I was regrouping from the trip and partly because I felt stress over the house. *"I'll start in the kitchen and get that under control."* I walked onto the porch, up and over the pile of dirt. *"No, first I'll get the shovel and dig out the entryway, and then I'll do the kitchen."* I went into the house. It could have been my imagination, but it even smelled messy. I know a meal tastes better when it looks good. I wonder if it's the same kind of deal with a house. Maybe a home smells better when it's neat.

"Hi ..." I called to Jeff and Ally. "Did Chris call to be picked up?"

Jeff answered, "Not yet, but Dad called! He said, 'Tell your mother, thanks!'"

"What?"

"Yeah, I think you're in trouble."

"I'm in trouble ... for what?"

"I don't know. Maybe you'd better call him."

"I will!"

"Hi, Mom," Ally chirped. Then her tone darkened. "Oh,

did Dad get ahold of you? He's furious! He came home to change his clothes 'cause when he was in court and he crossed his legs, ya know?"

"Yeah?"

"His skin showed."

"And that's supposed to be MY fault? Your father needs new clothes ... but he hates to go shopping! Is it my fault that he doesn't have much to choose from?"

"I don't know, Mom. I just know he's real mad."

"Yeah, well, I'm mad, too!"

The look on Ally's face made me feel guilty for dragging her into something that Danny and I should have settled privately.

"Never mind, Ally. I'll call Dad and we'll get this ironed out."

I jabbed out his number on my cordless and waited for the phone to ring. He answered.

"I understand you have a problem with me!" My enunciation was crisp and cool.

"Yes, I do. Is it too much to ask to have clean clothes in the closet?"

"Yes! Right now it is. I think your timing stinks! You know I've been out of town, and I've been working on a deadline. Things are a little behind."

"A little behind? The place is a pit! You've been home for three days, and you still haven't unpacked. You haven't been to the store; the yard is a trash hole from the dogs running wild.... I don't know what your problem is, but you sure seem to be spinning your wheels."

"You're right, Danny. You don't have a clue about what my problem is, because part of the problem is YOU!"

"Oh, sure. Blame YOUR disorganization on me! That's right. It's all MY fault!"

"I didn't say that. You're not listening!"

"Great, now I'm deaf! I'm tired of this conversation. The fact is, you really don't care. You let everything go until I can't stand it any more and I blow up. The kids are in their own little world, too. They know they're supposed to clean up after the dogs, but do they? You just try to walk across the lawn without slipping in one of the piles! Nobody cares. For days I've stepped over a styrofoam meat tray in the driveway, wondering how long it would stay there. If I didn't bend over and pick it up and put it in the garbage can myself, it'd be there forever." (I held back from telling him how much I'd LOVE to have been there when he bent over!)

"Danny, you say we're in our own little world, but you don't realize what that means. We've all got pressures beyond the garbage in the driveway. You act like the kids and I are a bunch of no-good, lazy, shiftless slackers!" (I dried the mouthpiece with my sleeve, took a deep breath, and continued.) "You're oblivious to what we all do while you're at work. Give some credit where it's due! You've always said, 'Homework comes first!' and they're on the honor roll. So the piles on the lawn don't always get attention. Well, evidently they've learned to prioritize between dog poop and good grades!

"Chris works five days a week at the pizza place; he swims on the team and plays tennis, and he goes to Civil Air Patrol once a week. And Jeff works weekends mowing lawns, and answers the phone at our office, and he practices with the diving team five nights a week.

"Now Ally, she's not old enough to get a job yet, but she helps me with dinner every night and does anything I ever ask her to do! She's student body president; she plays the piano and takes horseback riding lessons in Battle Ground two days a week—and who do you think carts them all over the place? When I'm not chauffeuring them to all THOSE places, I'm hauling them to the orthodontist or somewhere else they have to be, or I'm here at home trying to keep things up! If we missed the meat tray, we are sorry! But we are NOT a bunch of bums!"

"I didn't say you were bums. I'm only pointing out that the house is filthy."

"No, it isn't! It's very clean, and you know it! It's just a little messy."

"Okay, it's messy then. Call it what you want, but there isn't one room that looks clean. That's the way it goes. You let it keep getting worse until I explode, then you run around cleaning things up, and for a while you have the house in order, but then you get sidetracked and things are right back where they were."

"Excuse me? I get sidetracked? I get sidetracked because there are too many tracks, and I can't be on all of them at once! You think you're the only one who wants a clean house? Right now it's probably bothering me more than it's bothering you! I just have a longer fuse and more tolerance ... and I DON'T blame YOU for the circumstances that have led to the mess. That's where we're different! You hold ME responsible. Well, it's too much! I can't do it all any more!"

"Then figure it out and cut back."

"Cut back on what? The laundry, maybe? I think that's how this whole argument got started. What would you have me cut back on?"

"That's for you to figure out. I don't know your schedule. Just quit playing games and take care of it."

"Playing games ... that's wonderful!"

"You are. It's the poor-me game. Get serious and figure out some kind of a work schedule and then stick to it."

"Fine!" I swallowed back the tears. My throat hurt so much that the ache went deep into my chest as I mustered my last stand. "Danny, one more thing. The next time you have a grievance with me, DON'T deliver it through the children. It's certainly not fair to them, and it shows absolutely no respect for my position!"

I was proud of the way I had stood up for myself in

spite of the lump in my throat. I had spoken as articulately as William Buckley.

It was quiet.

"Yes ... I'm sorry about that. I was wrong."

I couldn't talk. The lump had my voice box in a squeeze.

"I'll see you tonight." His tone softened.

"Yeah." I slammed the AT&T into its cradle and let the tears burst.

How could he be so insensitive about my feelings? Quit playing the "poor-me game!" Humph! How could he put so little value on my efforts and my time? Why didn't he recognize my contribution and see that I'm not able to take care of the house and his needs the way I did before I started my business? He was acting like he thinks I don't care. Does he really believe that, or was it just a cheap shot? All HE seems to care about is "how does this affect me?" It affects him because I'm not there to cater to him, feed him, and wash his clothes! I don't expect HIM to wait on ME. I'd never think to call to him from the shower to see if he bought shampoo. I wouldn't dream of asking him to lay out an outfit for me to wear to a speech. I'd love to see the look on his face if I hollered from the bathroom, "Hey, Babe, lay out my burgundy suit, and put a shine on my black pumps. Oh, and I'll need my off-black pantyhose, and pick out a scarf while you're at it." Hah!

He knows the subject of organization is a touchy one with me, and how dare he throw the word "sidetracked" in my face? He knows that's the theme of one of my books! Figure out a work schedule and stick to it! Yeah, but don't figure him into it! I should have said, "How dare you even suggest that this is MY problem!" I should have told him to mind his own business! No, that's a cliché. I should have said, "Until you are ready to be reasonable, there is no point in discussing this any further."

Yeah, I should have used words like "perhaps" and "occasionally."

"Perhaps I am occasionally dilatory in my responsibilities, both in my business and at home. However, I am endeavoring to maintain a balance between the two and keep my mental, emotional, and physical vehicles intact."

No, he'd say, *"Stop playing the pseudo-intellectual game."* I can't believe he was so hateful. How could he attack me on my home front? He knows my family is the most important thing in my life. He just doesn't understand. That's all. Figure it out and cut back! Uh-huh! I oughta keep a time log of everything I do! Would he ever have his eyes opened!

I got a spurt of energy at the thought of making a list of my work load compared to his. I would make that list, and, at the next confrontation, I'd be ready! Meanwhile, I'd get the kids to help me straighten up the house.

In less than half an hour, the place looked terrific, proving my point that it was purely superficial clutter and not filth.

When Danny came home that night, we were coolly cordial. Polite, yet barely looking at each other, neither of us cared to take up where our phone conversation had left off. Both of us were overly pleasant to the children and obviously indifferent to each other. I was still fighting off hurt feelings and waves of tears. At the dinner table, I said I wasn't very hungry and excused myself. Sneaking a chicken leg from the platter in the kitchen, I took a paper towel, went to the bedroom, and ate the fowl in the dark.

It was only eight o'clock, but I was exhausted. The fight had worn me out. I positioned myself as far over on my side of the bed as I possibly could without dropping off the edge. I was determined to cling there all night. "Hmm!" I muttered to myself. "Cut back! I can think of ONE thing I'll be cutting back on, starting tonight!" I slept, but never so deeply as to risk drifting closer to the enemy. Danny kept on his edge, too.

In the morning, I got up without speaking. When I looked in the bathroom mirror, I scared myself. I noticed my cheek had what looked like a large, serious scar across it. (It was just an indentation from the cording on the edge of the mattress.) My eyes were puffy and bloodshot from crying myself to sleep, and there was a little bit of barbecue sauce from the chicken left on my chin.

I went into the kitchen to make coffee and noticed it was immaculate! *I'll bet the kids did the dishes for me. They'd do anything right now to ease the tension around here.*

"Are you and Dad still mad at each other?" Chris asked. He looked worried. Danny and I rarely argue, and our real fights are limited to about two a year: one in the spring when we launch the boat for the first trip of the season, and the other in the fall when we decide whether to sell it.

"Yeah, Chris, we're still mad, but we'll work it out. I could use your help, though. Dad seems to feel that no one cares about the house and the yard the way he does. I don't think that's true. I think we do care, but we're all so busy and we're going in so many different directions that it's hard to keep on top of everything."

"Yeah, I know."

"I'm going to talk to Jeff and Ally and get them to be more aware of picking up their things and helping with the laundry and dishes, but it's going to take all of us."

"Dad, too?"

"Yeah, Dad, too. But for right now, I think we should be concerned about our own habits."

"Okay." We hugged each other.

"Start this morning by sorting your laundry."

"Where should I put it, in the hall?"

"Uh ... no. I'll set up a place in the laundry room. The puppies are getting too big to be in there. It's time for them to go outside."

Ally came into the kitchen with a little cloud of concern over her head. "Are you and Dad fighting?"

"Hmm ... I think we already fought. Now we're thinking

about what we said to each other, and probably for a while we're both going to be upset."

"How come?"

"Because we agree there's a problem, but neither of us knows what to do about it yet. One thing I can tell you for sure ... I love your dad and he loves me. On a scale of one to ten, if one would be a dirty look and ten would be a divorce, this fight would only be about a five." (She didn't need to know that, during our phone fight, we were hovering around fifteen!) "You don't need to worry, but it would help if you would be extra careful to see that the house stays neat." She agreed.

Next Jeff confronted me. "How come Dad was so mad yesterday?" he pried.

"Because he looked bad, and he didn't know who to blame. His hair didn't work because we were out of shampoo; he needs new clothes ... I don't know ... the house was a mess. I've been gone and he's had to be both mother and father ... I think everything just came to a head at once and we both exploded."

"What do you need me to do?"

"Just make sure that you take care of your own messes. That alone will make a big difference."

"I will."

I easily had the support and cooperation of all three of the children. I praised them and acknowledged what each was already doing to help. Then we talked about what they could do to make things better around the house and easier for their father and me. I had to wonder why I wasn't able to talk to Danny in the same comfortable way I could talk to the children. Our conversation had been accusatory and hostile. Maybe it was because our egos were involved, but all we had succeeded in doing was to create bad feelings.

Ten

Less Than Friendly Persuasion

From Pam:
    When I left our office (we'd had to Federal Express the article to meet the deadline), I thought about the fight Peggy was going to have. Getting cooperation from her unsuspecting spouse of twenty years could be tricky. I was glad I didn't have to deal with that problem. Being single for ten years, I had promised myself that any man I became interested in would have to know, or at least be willing to learn, basic homemaking skills, before I would ever consider marriage.

It was true that most of the men I'd encountered were pathetic in that area. (Peggy and I had considered teaching a beginner's homemaking class for men only, after I'd gone through a string of retarded male homemakers. We agreed, however, that most men wouldn't come to a class like that unless we held it in a tavern, served beer and pretzels, and had wide-screen sports at the breaks.)

Terry was the new man in my life, and he was certainly no exception to the domestic retardation I'd seen in my previous dates. I liked him a lot and was seriously working on improving his skill level, because I could see his potential.

I had invited him over for dinner, and, because it would be his first meal in my home, I had decided to be extra careful that the evening's work load would be equal. I even called him at his office and told him we would be going to the supermarket together before we made dinner. He was pleased with the pronoun "we," and he agreed to take off a little early to allow time for the shopping.

We had fun together at the store, though I felt a bit as if I were taking a kindergartner on a field trip. Here was a forty-four-year-old man who had been single for two years and was feeding primarily on canned soup and peanut butter sandwiches.

The produce section was as foreign to him as the underside of a car would be to me. Interestingly, he soaked up every bit of information I gave out as we passed the colorful variety of fruits and vegetables. He was pleased to know that he could buy just one or two potatoes instead of a ten-pound sack. When we came to the bananas, I chose a nice yellow bunch and tore it in half, putting three in the cart. He had a look on his face as if he'd just witnessed a bank holdup.

"You can do that!?" he whispered, as he wielded a guilty glance around the produce department to see if anyone had seen me.

"You mean rip a bunch of bananas apart?"

"Yeah ... that's really okay to do?" He was still nervous, as if he'd been an accomplice in a crime.

"Of course it's okay to do that. What did you think would happen: sirens, loudspeakers: 'Guy in produce, rippin' off bananas?'"

He liked what I had told him and stripped off one more banana to test the validity of what he had learned. No sirens ... no loudspeakers ... no irate produce manager ... It really WAS okay!

With the bananas behind us, I asked him to get some carrots, celery, lettuce, and a couple of pounds of broccoli while I finished getting the fruit. He took the shopping cart and headed for the greens.

When I was finished with my selections, I joined him. He looked anxious for my approval as he cocked his head sideways a couple of times, motioning me to check the cart. "I got everything you told me to." He beamed.

I beamed back and turned to put my fruit with his vegetables. I was mortified to see what he had done! He had torn a head of romaine lettuce in half, severed four stalks of celery from the rest of their family, and decapitated all the broccoli florets from their stems, leaving the heavy stalks next to the scale. It was so unbelievable that my mouth started moving before my ability to edit what was coming out could take over. A flurry of superlatives hit Terry in the face.

When my social-awareness alarm caught up with my tongue, I was embarrassed, and Terry looked like a dog that didn't know why he was in trouble. He needed more hands-on training ... but not in public. I wondered if I could get him a video on grocery store etiquette that he would view in the privacy of his own home.

Leaving the spoils behind, I reluctantly rolled him into the meat department. I rang the bell for the butcher.

"What does that do?"

I hate sarcasm, but I couldn't resist. "It rings the butcher, who lives in the back with all his little barnyard friends. When he hears the bell, he'll come out and we'll tell him that we want this chicken sawed in half."

"In half? Why?" he winced.

"Well, because we are going to barbecue it. After it's in

half, we'll take it home and put the halves on the grill.
Then the meat will cook from the inside out." I was beginning to feel the superiority of my vast culinary knowledge.

The butcher appeared, looking as though he'd been on
the front lines. I was amused that he knew I was the one
who had interrupted his work, even though Terry had the
chicken in his hand. "What can I do ya for, ma'am?"

Terry held the chicken out as if he were holding a dead
possum he'd found on the freeway, and gestured, with a
slicing motion, to cut the bird in half. "We'd like this cut in
two pieces, please." His voice was definite and authorita-
tive.

"Whoa! You want it cut that way?" (Terry's cutting
motion had divided the hen's top from its bottom.) "Which
one of you guys is gonna get the butt and the two legs?"
The butcher laughed. "I'm a breast man, myself! How
'bout you?"

Terry laughed, too.

I interrupted their obnoxious fun over the chicken
parts, took the package out of Terry's hand, and instructed,
"Just cut it right, please."

We were in the store much too long.

At home, I had Terry light the charcoal. (I made a mental note of the time it took.) When he was through watching the flames and was sure the briquettes were going to
burn, he went out to the street to get the newspaper.

I let him sit down long enough to get comfortable. "Ter-
rrrry!" I called from the kitchen.

"What?" He sounded as if he were responding to a lilt-
ing request.

"Will you please make the salad?"

It was interesting to find out that his idea of a salad was
chopped lettuce. I was stunned to discover that his idea of
salad dressing was mayonnaise. Not even mayo and cat-
sup; just mayonnaise. I enlightened him. We made Caesar
salad together.

I saw to it that the meal preparations were absolutely equal. By the time we were ready to eat, I was hoarse from the cooking lesson, and he was much more aware of what goes into fixing a good dinner. The paper was never read, but we set the table together and took turns basting the chicken. Terry snipped half the beans and learned how to clarify butter. I cut up my half of the strawberries, and, while he sliced his, I showed him how to make the roux. We shared in the preliminary cleanup, and when we sat down to eat he was exhausted and had almost lost his appetite.

After the meal, he was ready to throw himself back on the couch and relax. That's when the flare-up occurred.... There were still dishes to do.

The next morning, I called my sister. "I think a class to get men to do half is a generation away. Terry left last night with the look of a freed slave, and I don't think he'll call for a while, either; at least not until he recuperates from the big dinner! You know what? I hate being demanding. I get help with the housework only because I resort to screaming and nagging. The kids oblige, but it's always a big fight. And now Terry ... I'm sure I'm listed in his little black book under 'B' instead of 'Y.'

"The darned thing about that is I love to cook, and I would've rather done it myself. It's relaxing to me. I feel creative. I love the appreciation for a fabulous meal ... but I was afraid if I let him sit there and read the paper, he'd get the idea that HIS place was in the LA-Z-BOY! Isn't THAT interesting? They don't make a LA-Z-Girl recliner!"

"Oh, brother!"

"I don't want to end up with a man who's unwilling to do his share. Maybe I was wrong to insist we do everything together. It would have been all right if I had cooked alone, as long as he helped with the cleanup. I hate to do the dishes after I've cooked. But who doesn't? I mean, do you know anyone who finds 'cleanup' fulfilling? I'll bet the women's liberation movement was started by a bunch of homemakers who got sick and tired of cleaning up after everybody.

"I hope I didn't scare Terry away with my equal rights crusade. Do you think he'll call me? ... Hello? ... Sissy, are you in there?"

"No, I'm not! Here I've been in love with a man for two decades, and I found out his devotion is only as deep as a pile of dirty laundry! You're asking me if I think Terry will call you? Quite frankly, Charlotte, I don't give a rip!"

"Well!"

"Oh, I'm sorry, Sissy ... I'm just upset. Danny and I had a huge fight last night."

"Ohhhh ... right, I forgot about you guys! Did you win?"

"No. But neither did he. We're at a stalemate. We're speaking, but there is definitely a chill in the air!"

"What are you going to do?"

"I don't know yet. We'll have to talk it out sooner or later. I'm not looking forward to it. Have you ever had to argue with a policeman?"

"No."

"It's a losing deal! Danny puffs up and his lips disappear."

"I think all men do that when they're mad."

"Well, it's very intimidating."

"I know it!"

"I'm not going to get into any arguments until I have all my facts. I'm going to keep a log to show just exactly how I spend my day, compared to his. He may put in three or four more hours at his office than I do, but when he comes home, that's it! It's rest and relaxation. I come home in time to chauffeur the kids all over town, make dinner, clean up, do some laundry, and then it's bedtime!"

"Oh, Sissy, it'll be obvious that you do way more than he does."

"Yeah. But, you know, Danny is a hard worker. I don't mean to sound like he doesn't do anything, because that's not true. He has totally remodeled the house, and his flowerbeds are impeccable. What gets me is that he leaves all the little day-in and day-out responsibilities to me. It's the things that SEEM insignificant but collectively keep everything working that he takes for granted. He doesn't notice until one of the 'little' things doesn't get done, and THEN it gets his attention. Maybe he'd be more appreciative if he was responsible for some of those little things himself. Before I confront him, I'm going to have a list of changes to negotiate."

"Like what?"

"Like I don't want to make his sack lunch any more. On the weekends, I don't want to make breakfast both mornings. I want him to make it on Saturday and I'll do it on Sunday. I don't want to make the bed after he gets out of it, and I want him to clean his own tub ring and wash his whiskers out of the sink.

"I think we should take turns taking and picking up the kids. I want him to do his own dishes and supervise the kitchen cleanup while I relax from cooking the meal. I want him to share the laundry responsibility, take turns going to the cleaners ... and I don't EVER want to wrestle the German shepherds, trying to get them to the vet again. They're just too big!

"I'm going to have all of this in writing. It's going to be in black and white so there's no misunderstanding."

"Do you think you'll cry?"

"Yes."

"Darn. Men hate tears!"

"I know, but I'm not going to worry about it. In fact, I'm going to plan the talk so that I can cry hard if I feel like it."

"Whoa!"

"Yeah, but I don't cry very often, so if I need to cry over this, I get to. It'd be different if I was sloppin' all over the house in tears every day. THESE tears will mean something."

"Good luck!"

We hung up and I sat at my desk, so grateful that I was single. I had to admit that in my middle years, I had become very cynical about men. My son, Mike, had recently warned me that I had more of a chance of being sniped by a terrorist than I had of ever remarrying! (Peggy told me I should start dating terrorists.) Quite frankly, I was in no hurry to do ANY knot-tying! I thought about Terry. *Wouldn't it be great if, when you got married, the guy came with a written guarantee stating that, if he didn't work out, you could take him back and get a new one?* The thought of it made me laugh and prompted me to specify my spousal requirements in a poem.

WARRANTY MAN

You can bet that my next husband
Will come with a warranty.

Thirty years on parts and service,
He'll be trouble-free.

I will read that operator's manual
To figure out how he'll work.

I'll find out how to turn him on
And disconnect him when he's being a jerk.

I won't have to jump-start
His worn-out battery,

And if he starts to smoke,
He's going back to the factory.

I'll take all the extras,
As far as options go.

He's gotta have a nice size trunk
And be equipped with booze control.

I'll take him in for tune-ups;
They'll check his plugs and points.

They'll test his shock absorbers
And grease up his ball joints.

And when his road of life has ended,
I'll tow him faithfully,

Back to where he came from,
With a money-back guarantee.

Eleven

Infraction's the Name of the Game

From Peggy:
My warfare with Danny was far from over. Underneath the dirty laundry, there were deeply rooted male/female issues that needed to be weeded out and done away with forever.

I'm not sure when women got stuck with total responsibility for the home. I have my own theory that it goes back more than six million years. I think that in the beginning there was equality; male and female in perfect symmetry. Harmonious, even, and well-balanced, the two were distinct without difference. Like two pieces in a jigsaw puzzle, opposite yet perfectly matched, the equivalents were complete ... and then came mealtime. The dialogue went something like this:

"Great night's sleep! I'm hungry. Are you?"

"Yeah, I guess so. My stomach feels kinda funny. Maybe I just need to eat."

"Do you want me to go out and get something while you keep the fire going?"

"It doesn't matter. I could go."

"Nah, your stomach's acting up. I'll go."

"Okay, you go get it, and I'll cook it when you get back."

"Sounds fair to me."

"Good. I'll clean up around the cave and set the table."

"Great!"

He left in search of food, and she stayed home and kept the cave warm. Outside, there were all kinds of scary, scaly beasts and giant flying vegetarians, and food wasn't that easy to find. Meanwhile, back at the cave, the fire started to smoke, the queasy stomach got worse, and cavern-to-cavern solicitors kept the pregnant entity from getting a nap. Returning exhausted, the huntsman with the food was annoyed. He felt that she didn't appreciate all he'd been through out in the world. She also felt aggravated. The cave was boring and smoky, he was later than he'd said he'd be, the food didn't satisfy the craving, and the firewood was almost gone.

"How was your day?"

"Oh, just terrific. It's one big party out there."

"Yeah? Well, it wasn't that great being stuck here all day, either!"

Day in and day out, the couple woke up, got the food, cleaned the cave, cooked, ate, argued, and turned in for the night. Soon they were blessed with a child. The mysterious birth thrilled the co-creators, but with the added mouth to feed, the designated food-finder felt pressured to bring back even more. He began to leave earlier and stay out longer in search of provisions. After a tough day, he would often stop at a popular watering hole to enjoy the company of his fellow hunters. Commiserating over losses or swapping tales of brave victories, he'd usually lose track of time. Staggering home, dragging the catch of the day behind him, he would be greeted by his less than festive spouse.

While the father was out foraging, the mother nurtured the little cavette, teaching her right from wrong and the art of homemaking. The child tore around the cave, making messes, noise, and trouble. Every year there was another child. When it became clear what was causing the pregnancies, the stretch-marked female and the hairy-chested male had to cut back on their only form of entertainment (except for an occasional game of Pictionary).

When the cave got too crowded, the mother said to the father, "Take your sons with you today. The girls and I will clean the cave." Before anyone realized it, the roles were established ... the male went out into the world and the female kept up the cave. The balance didn't start shifting until "Family Ties" and "The Cosby Show" were in the top ten.

Thursday, March 26, 1987, was a beautiful, fresh, sunny spring morning, except at the Joneses'. I was gray. I hated the way I felt. I was bitter and hurt, fragile and confused. I wanted to get out of the house. I borrowed Chris's Walkman, plugged myself into something classical (leaving Def Leppard on Chris's desk), and Rosie and I went for a walk. She needed to get away, too.

I live on the edge of a canyon, overlooking a lake and wildlife refuge. There is a paved path around the lake that winds through maple and evergreen trees and peacefully leaves the world behind. It's a perfect place to listen for answers to prayer. (I know you probably didn't buy this book in a religious bookstore, and the last thing you want to hear is a sermon, but if I don't say that I prayed for an answer to the problems I was having at home, there will be a hole in the telling of what happened to make things right.)

I let Rosie off her leash, and she ran ahead to drink and flounce around in the creek. Then I sat down on a big rock, and I prayed. "I don't know what to do, God. These feelings of bitterness and anger are choking me. I feel heavy and dark in my spirit. I can't see any light in this situation. I can't even look at Danny without getting mad!

I've gone over and over the phone fight, and his words are more piercing every time. I need peace and a simple answer. I want us to understand each other. Please help me, God."

"Hey, you! Is that your German sheperd?"

"Huh?" I opened my eyes and saw Rosie in the distance. She had treed a jogger! I ran to rescue the terrified man. "Rosie! Heel! Heel! Rosie, heel! She won't hurt you; she's just smelling you! Rose! Bad dog!" The man was frozen to the tree and speechless. "There, see, she's back on her leash. You can come down now. I'm so sorry she scared you! Are you all right?"

"If you ever walk this trail with that wild animal off his leash again, I'll call the cops so fast you won't have a prayer!"

I felt like Jimmy Stewart did after he'd prayed on Christmas Eve in *It's a Wonderful Life*.

The naughty dog and I walked back home, and although my heart was even heavier, the exercise and fresh air had felt good. The only answer I had seemed to hear was one word: "Rest." I hadn't slept well since the fight. He was right; I needed a nap.

Later that day, I was on my way to the store, still preoccupied with thoughts of my forty-eight-hour domestic battle. The kids were being extra careful to see that their things were put away, but I knew it would last only as long as the cold war Danny and I were waging. Once the smoke cleared, things would pile up again, and I'd go right back to nagging and policing.

Just as I was thinking that it was a shame nobody was accountable without a fight, I noticed an abandoned car alongside the freeway. The highway patrol had tagged it. (Danny told me once that they tag cars before they tow them. The bright ticket is a signal to other circling troopers that the vehicle has been checked out, written up, and earmarked for the hook. I think he said the owner has something like twenty-four hours to retrieve the lemon before Speedy's Tow Masters get it.)

I wondered what it would cost the guy. *Hmm ... too bad we don't have some kind of house patrol. Stuff left out would get tagged, and the owner would have just so much time to retrieve it without paying. Not a bad idea ... make it official just like the state patrol does. Make the rules and then enforce them.* I got excited. There was the simple answer I had asked for in my prayer.

While I was in the store, I bought a package of bright, fluorescent adhesive dots the size of a nickel. When I got home, I couldn't wait! I went through the house and put a dot on anything I found that had been left out. (Anything of mine I found I quietly put away!) I was delighted that, since the children and I had made tidiness our life's work for the last couple of days, most of the stickers appeared on Danny's things! I loved it! His tennis bag was in the entry hall, his shoes were under the coffee table, the newspaper was on the couch, his coffee mug was on the bathroom counter, his sunglasses were on top of the dresser, his Thermos was by the sink, and his sport coat was hung on the back of the kitchen chair. With pleasure, I tagged him in every room. The children watched me.

"What are you doing with those stickers, Mom? Are we going to have another garage sale?" Jeff was puzzled. "How come Dad's selling his good coat?"

"He's not. I'm just tagging it for being on the chair." As I made my final rounds, my inquisitive kids followed me.

"See all these things your father left out? I have decided to play a little game with him. You can play it, too. The main rule is, if it's not decorative, it shouldn't be out. If it's out, I will consider it abandoned and tag it as an infraction!"

"What's an infraction?" Ally asked.

"You know, it's like a ... violation."

"What about your stuff?"

"Huh?"

"Won't Dad tag you for your stuff?"

"Uh ... sure, that's only fair. However, as you can see, all of mine is put away." There was arrogance in my tone.

"Mom?"

"Yes, Chris."

"I don't think your purse is a very good decoration on the piano."

"Well, no, but it's my purse, and I need to be able to leave it out. You understand."

"Not really. If the main rule is that junk left out has to be a decoration or be put away, I think you'd better find another place for your purse or you'll get tagged for it." (I put my purse in the hall closet on the shelf. It was the last time I would ever have to look for it again!)

The kids and I talked about the new game in more detail, making up the rules as we thought of them. Infractions would be counted for laundry and dishes left in bedrooms or any place else (one infraction per item), beds unmade, lights left on when the room is empty, tub rings, toilet seats left up, and coats, purses, books, and anything else left out that shouldn't have been.

Since I had more time in the morning than anyone else, I said I'd empty the dishwasher first thing, so they could put their breakfast dishes in there. If they left them in the sink when the dishwasher was empty, they would be counted as infractions. The owner would have a reasonable amount of time to retrieve his or her belongings without penalty. We would write the time on the dot so there would be no arguments about how long items had been left out.

When the time limit expired, the infractions and the amount charged would be written on 3 × 5 cards (one for each person in the family) and posted on the bulletin board in the kitchen. We decided that twenty-five cents was a fair amount to charge for each item and agreed that, for one week, we would be on probation, adding up the money but not actually collecting it. It would give us a chance to be aware of how much our actions would cost us, once the game really started.

INFRACTION CARD FOR ———————————————		
DATE	INFRACTION	BALANCE
		TOTAL ———

Then we discussed what we should do with the money. I thought it should go toward something decorative for the house (with all our junk put away, I could see the need for some tasteful knickknacks).

"What's the object?" Chris asked.

"To have the house neat," I said.

"I think the object oughta be to win the money by having the fewest infractions. The clean house would just be a by-product," Jeff proposed.

I wasn't sure I liked the logic of my brilliant offspring. I wished that he cared more about a clean house and less about the money, but the other kids loved his idea.

We decided that we could all act as watchmen and tag each other. We called the game Infraction! (I opted not to explain this new idea to Danny for a while. Wicked as it may have been, I wanted to infract him as many times as I could. It would be evidence of his contribution to the mess and I would have it in black and white ... and fluorescent red.)

During the next two days, we filled our 3 × 5 infraction cards with violations. (In one week, there would have been $19.75 in our kitty if we had actually collected the money.) The first day, Ally had eleven bathroom infractions alone. After that, she rarely left anything out that we could tag. Chris left ice cream bowls in his room, and Jeff couldn't seem to get his backpack out of the hall each day after school. I was repeatedly tagged on my car keys, which soon joined my purse in the closet, and I also got penalized for leaving my watch on the windowsill. (My watch is pretty, but they ruled that it was personally decorative rather than publicly decorative.)

Unbeknown to him, Danny was racking up the most violations. The times that he noticed dots on his things, he unconsciously peeled them off with no more concern than he'd have about picking a cat hair off his coat. He was guilty of whiskers, tub rings, toilet seats, damp towels, dishes, mugs, mail, and more. Since he was such a substantial contributor to the pot, we all looked forward to the day he'd find out he was a player and have to cough up the cash. I was second in line for the clutter crown; Jeff and Chris were tied for third (and eventually formed a union whereby they agreed not to infract each other and split the money, should they ever win it), and, after the first day, Ally was the neatest.

For the short time that the kids and I had been on the new system, the house had never looked so consistently tidy. The impact of something so simple was shocking. It had been so easy to enforce, yet its power was incredible. I wished that we hadn't created it out of desperation but instead had run into it happily, in some how-to book, without having to go through the fire.

Danny was still in the dark about the dots. I'd seen him pick one of the colored tattlers off of the seat of his pants (which had been carelessly tossed over a chair), and I thought that he must surely be puzzled by its conspicuous grip on his backside. He had no idea what the little fluorescent dot meant or how much it would cost him in the future. I loved it!

It was Saturday morning, and Pam and I were supposed to give a luncheon speech on "Home Is Where the Heart Is." My heart wasn't in it. When a couple doesn't usually fight, a blowup like the one Danny and I had had was especially debilitating. We both wanted a truce.

"We need to talk," Danny finally said. (Since I had suffered the most injustice, I felt that it was appropriate that he made the first advance toward peace.)

"Yes, I know we do, but when we talk, we need to have time to get everything that's bothering us out in the open. I know I'm going to cry hard, and I need to be able to do that without worrying about wrecking my makeup."

"All right."

"If it's okay with you, I'd like to postpone the talk until after my speech."

"That's fine. When will you be home?"

"About two."

"I'll be here."

I had had time to think, and so had he. We were both prepared for the confrontation. At two o'clock we met in our bedroom, closed the door, sat on the bed, and squared off. (I was glad that I was dressed up and looked my best. He didn't look that good.) It's hard to argue with a policeman, but it's probably just as difficult to have a talk with someone who earns her living giving speeches and writing books. The "talk" took two hours.

"I'm sorry for the things I've been thinking about you," I confessed.

"So what's going on?"

"I've given it a lot of thought and I've really prayed about it, because I want to understand both sides. I think there are several things happening to us right now."

"Like what?"

"I feel like you take me for granted. It doesn't seem like you appreciate all the things I do for you and the family. You're quick to point out what I haven't done and slow to notice what I have."

"So are you."

"What? In what way?" (It was news to me!)

"Last Saturday, for instance, I spent all day in the yard on my day off while you were shopping, and you came home and didn't even notice."

"I did, too! I told you it looked real nice."

"Yeah, well, maybe I would have felt like you really meant it if you'd taken a minute to walk around and really look at it."

"You're right. I should have, and I was going to come back out as soon as I took my packages in, but then I got busy and forgot. I'm sorry. I guess we both do that. The other day I was so proud of myself for hemming your new jeans right away and I said, 'Guess what, Danny! Your new jeans are hemmed and ready to wear!' and you said, 'Good. Did you sew up the pocket in my jacket?' I needed way more points for that!"

"I'm sorry. I'll try to be more appreciative."

"So will I."

"So what else? He took out his pipe and started his tamping ritual (a sign that he was vulnerable and needed the motions to give him time to think).

"I want you to lighten up."

He stared at me.

"You're always finding what's wrong." (I countered his tamping with some nail filing.) "Like Saturday, after you and the boys worked so hard all day in the yard, you stood back and looked at what you'd done and Chris said, 'It sure looks good, huh, Dad?' and you said, 'Yeah, but it needs barkdust.' I saw Chris and Jeff just look at each other."

"Really? Well, I didn't mean that I didn't appreciate

how much they did. I could just see what else we still had
to do."

"You do it a lot. Someone will say, 'Dad, the pool sure
looks great!' and you'll say, 'Yeah, but we need to scrub the
tiles!' If you could just stop yourself before you say, 'Yeah,
but ...'"

"I don't mean to do that. It's just that there's always
something that needs to be done."

"I know, and that's the point. When you say, 'We can't
play until the work is done,' you forget that the work is
NEVER done! So where's the time for fun?"

"Hmm ..."

"I watched you last summer with the pool. You
scrubbed it, vacuumed it, chlorinated it, backwashed it,
and tested it constantly, but did you ever swim?"

"Not very much."

"You need to kick back and play more."

"Sometimes it irritates ME that you can play no matter
what needs to be done. Remember when the McLains
called and asked us to go on a picnic to Lewisville Park?
You were right in the middle of wallpapering the little
bathroom, but you said, 'Sure! We'd love to go!' I couldn't
believe it! I wish you would take things a little more seriously."

"We're so different from each other, aren't we?"

"Yep. That's probably why, after twenty years, we're still
intrigued with each other."

We were making progress, but there was still the issue
of work loads to be discussed. I had abandoned the idea of
throwing a time log in Danny's face because I decided I
didn't have to prove my value that way, to him or anyone
else!

Initially I had divided a piece of notebook paper in half
lengthwise, with his name at the top of one side and mine
at the top of the other, but, staring at the blank college
rule, I changed my mind. I wasn't afraid to align my day

with his, hour by hour; I just hated the nitpicky thought of, *Okay, let's see, it's 6:15. I'm making the coffee and what is HE doing? Ah ha! Still in bed, I see. LOG IT!*

I also hated it because of the ramifications of the hourly comparison. I could just hear what he'd be thinking: *It's 12:45 and I don't have the time to stop and eat! I wonder what SHE is doing. I think I'll call her at the office. "Hi, is Peggy there? She's at the Chat 'n' Chew? When did she leave? ... 11:30?"* (Very interesting!) *"Would you have her call me when her lunch hour and a half is over?"* I'll log in exactly how many minutes she spent eating!

Danny has no idea of how often I take a long lunch, spoiling my appetite and allowing me to give the impression at dinner that I eat like a bird. Depending on which day was being logged, the work load scale could tip in my favor or not. Some days, Danny works overtime or goes out of town, and he doesn't get home again until the next day or even the next week. That is the nature of his job. Other days, I'm the one who has to work late or travel. It would be very difficult to determine who is working the hardest, because we both work hard.

Apart from each other, we live completely different lives. He deals with all the ugliness in the world, and I'm a humorist. We couldn't be more opposite. If we were totally honest with each other, we would admit that neither of us really knows what the other's day is like. We do know that we wouldn't trade places with each other for anything!

Danny can't imagine how I can get up in front of a thousand people and give a speech, or go on television and not faint. He says it would scare him more than raiding an outlaw biker's party. (One time when he had to give the crime report on the local radio station, he said it was ninety seconds of hell! Unable to think of the word *deceased*, he said, "We are investigating the identity of the ... ah ... dead fellow." He was embarrassed!)

On the other hand, if I had to do the things Danny has

had to do, like wade through the filth of a drug dealer's house, wrestle a vomiting drunk into my car, hold a dying man's hand, break up a fight between a man and his wife, rescue a baby from a burning house, shoot a hit-and-run bank robber, go to an autopsy, or investigate a murder ... I couldn't!

One thing we do have in common is that we both know the feeling of working our faces off, with no rewards or applause. I have seen Danny's frustration at the end of a day when he has nothing to show for all of his efforts. He can work a case for months, finally arrest the crook, do all the paperwork, and, on the way home, pass the prisoner on the freeway because he's been released on bail or the jails are too crowded. Like homemaking, police work can be a thankless, losing battle.

I was sure that Danny admired my work from a distance, the same as I respected what he was doing. Still, I didn't think he would appreciate all the time I spent visiting with my sister. On a time log, it wouldn't look that good. I was afraid Danny wouldn't recognize the value of those "visits," even though they inevitably earned us a substantial amount of money. When we were together, we came up with our most profound thoughts, humorous viewpoints, and creative ideas, which turned into books, speeches, and television appearances. Was it our fault that we had so much fun while we worked? Maybe some things just weren't fair. Back home, at least, they weren't, and I was about to show my husband my new ideas for changing things on the home front. Perhaps what I wanted, almost more than a fifty-fifty deal, was appreciation for what I was doing to make our home an oasis from the world outside. I was doing more than Danny realized, and in his unknowingness he had been insensitive. We continued our talk.

"So what else?" he said.

"Have you noticed how neat the house has been lately?" I asked.

"Yes, I have, and I've wondered how long it will last."

Wanting to rip his tongue out, but containing myself for a more incisive victory, I deliberately put down my nail file, folded my hands, and proceeded to explain our new infraction game. With a feeling of importance, I presented him with his personal list of infractions for the last couple of days ($9.75 worth), then graciously reassured him that it was merely a probationary week, so he needn't actually pay.

I showed him, in writing, how his messes contributed to the conditions he so disliked. It was the first time he was aware that HIS stuff was cluttering the house as much as my unpacked suitcase had. He had to admit that the object of the game (lowest infractee takes all) was a most brilliant money twist, and the by-product of a clutter-free house was even more appealing.

"So, Danny, do I have your support?"

"Sure, I'll play."

With clutter out of the way, we moved on to the more delicate issue of his contribution to household responsibilities. I got to say all the things I had practiced on my sister and rehearsed in my mind. I didn't leave out a word, and I had his complete attention when I said, "It's no longer men's work or women's work! It is people-who-live-in-the-house work!" At one point, I had to ask Danny to relax his lips from an angry line and unfold his arms. He asked me to stop pointing at him and to contralto my voice.

"Can I read something to you?" I was holding some papers in my hand. "It's about Christmas." He had a pained look on his face, as if he were about to listen to an Edgar Allan Poe poem.

"Sure."

"It's a list of all the things that, traditionally, fall in a mother's lap." He listened as I read all the things that had to be done:

- Make a list of the holiday and family traditions to be followed
- Take the children to see Santa Claus
- Go caroling
- Find out what children and family members want for Christmas
- Make gift list for family, friends, neighbors, col leagues, employees, children's gifts to family, friends, and teachers
- Select gifts that must be mailed early
- Buy gifts that must be mailed early
- Take children shopping so that they can pick out their presents for each other, parents, grandparents, and teachers
- Mail the gifts
- Buy remainder of gifts (including extra gifts for those you forgot who might drop in)
- Buy stocking stuffers
- Buy wrapping paper, ribbons, gift cards, and tape
- Wrap the gifts
- Make card list (save for next year)
- Buy cards
- Address cards
- Buy stamps
- Mail early
- Rearrange furniture
- Order tree
- Pick up tree
- Buy and hang wreath
- Check decorations (crèche, tree stand)
- Check tree lights (replace bulbs)
- Make decorations (string popcorn and cranberries, make tree ornaments)
- Buy decorations (bulbs, tinsel, hooks)
- Trim the tree

- Clean the house
- Buy and arrange holly, mistletoe, flowers, and pine boughs
- Set up the candles
- Decorate the house (yard and outside the house)
- Place gifts under the tree
- Hang and stuff stockings
- Leave a snack for Santa near the tree
- Give tips, gifts, thanks, and appreciation to special people (milkman, mailman, paperboy, employees, garbage collector, hairdresser)
- Check after-holiday sales on Christmas gifts for next year.
- Remember the needy and donate to your favorite charity

"And now, Danny, you're finished, unless, of course, like last year, we're going to have another Christmas party. Then you need to:

- Decide on the date and the time
- Plan the guest list
- Write out directions to the house and duplicate it
- Call the guests
- Buy the stamps
- Send out the invitations and directions
- Plan the menu
- Make shopping list
- Order special holiday food (goose, seafood, plum pudding)
- Assess the need for a caterer or other help and hire
- Borrow/rent/buy tables, chairs, coatrack, bar, cof feemaker
- Wash/borrow/rent/buy dishes, cups, serving dishes, and punch bowl

- Wash/borrow/rent/buy glasses (wine, champagne, eggnog, punch)
- Polish/borrow/rent/buy silverware
- Polish trays and silver items (candlesticks and candy dishes
- Clean table linens, dish towels, and aprons
- Take out the napkin rings
- Refill salt and pepper shakers
- Prepare an outfit to be worn
- Check recipes for procedures to be done in advance
- Buy ingredients for special holiday treats (fruitcakes, candy, and cookies)
- Buy holiday candles
- Buy the beverages
- Replenish the bar with condiments and supplies (onions, olives, cherries, lemons, limes, oranges, and stirrers)
- Buy mixers and juices
- Buy film and flashbulbs
- Buy paper goods (paper towels, napkins, and toilet paper)
- Shop for the food
- Get money to cover all the expenses
- Make the ice
- Chill the beverages
- Make a list of cooking and serving chores
- Make holiday drinks (eggnogs and toddies)
- Prepare foods that can be made ahead of time
- Put out the guest towels
- Clear out the closet and set up a coatrack
- Prepare a place for boots and umbrellas
- Check outdoor lighting
- Load the camera
- Put out ashtrays and coasters
- Buy last-minute perishables

- Buy the flowers and make a centerpiece
- Cook
- Set the table
- Put out the ice bucket, tongs, condiments, and snacks
- Make the juices for the drinks
- Decant the wine
- Set up the coffeemaker and the teapot
- Prepare the sugar bowl, creamer, lemons, and teabags
- Put out the ice
- Heat up the toddies
- Set out the hors d'oeuvres
- Warm and prepare the serving dishes
- Serve and clean as you go
- Return the rented/borrowed items

"See, I do Christmas every year, and your part is licking envelopes! That's not fair."

"I guess not, but I can tell you, we'll never have another Christmas party! That's insanity!"

"And listen to this. There's another list in here for packing for a summer vacation...."

"Okay! Okay! Okay! I get the picture. What do you want me to do?"

"I want you to do your half."

It was the beginning of new awareness for my husband, and from that time on things were very different. In the next weeks, we redefined the game to cover gray areas, such as personal bedrooms. In the name of relaxation, the resident needed to be able to kick back and leave out a little, but we agreed that no laundry, dishes, trash, or unmade beds would be allowed.

To keep the children from nosing around each other's bedrooms and our own, in search of violations, we added an invasion-of-privacy clause, whereby minors were not permitted to infract anything in another person's bedroom. Only parental tagging in those rooms would be permitted.

We learned, in time, that if the infraction cards came down, so did the house. As embarrassing as it was, the degree of neatness in our home depended on the 3 x 5s on the bulletin board. We were accountable because of cash, but at least we were accountable.

(We also discovered that, if the losers didn't fork over the money within twenty-four hours, they got away without paying, because everybody was concentrating on the next week's game. We made a new rule to stop the boys from cheating their sister out of her due. If payment, in cash, wasn't received within twenty-four hours of the verified tally, players would owe double the amount, compounded daily.)

With Danny's input, the game was even more fun. We continued to make new rulings, like time-outs for illness, holidays, and vacations, and seventy-two-hour amnesty for schoolbooks left out during finals. A shower lasting more than seven minutes was declared a misdemeanor, stopping hot water hogs cold!

After playing the game for several weeks, we added the car and the yard ... and Styrofoam meat trays in the driveway were a thing of the bitter past.

Twelve

Keeping Up with the Joneses

From Pam:

Before I decided to try the infraction cards at my house, I watched Peggy and her family for more than four months. It was amazing how consistently tidy her house was. Each person had taken responsibility for his or her own belongings, and Danny had assumed a good portion of the household tasks. The yard, which had always looked good, was even neater because the whole family was doing their part.

It was summer now, and I was back to being a single mother with three children in the house. Mike and Peggy Ann were home from college and busy with their summer jobs. I knew if I didn't get control soon, I would once again experience a summer full of stress. I'd barely made it through spring break with a voice.

Terry did call me back after he had rested from dinner at my house, and we started seeing each other almost every day. We had met when we were thirteen. We'd gone through junior high school and high school together, and although we had never dated, we had always been good friends. We were cheerleading partners for three years in high school and spent hours with each other, practicing our routines with the rally squad. We were together every Friday night because there was always a game. Our scrapbooks have many pictures of us together ... because we always were. Now we were spending wonderful hours, remembering our happy days and planning new ones.

One night we were having dinner in a very romantic setting, discussing how compatible we were, when he said something that abruptly changed the tone of the evening. "I can see that there is a little difference in the way you live and the way I do." He looked as if he hoped I was listening.

"Really, and what is that?" I could feel a judgment coming my way, and I silently reminded myself that I take criticism very easily.

"I have noticed that you and your kids leave quite a bit of stuff out at your house." Mysteriously, he seemed to look like my mother for an instant.

Even though I knew it was generally true, I wanted him to be specific. "Like what, for instance?"

"Oh, like the blanket Joanna took when we went to watch the fireworks. It's August. The blanket has been in the entryway for over three weeks."

I suddenly knew how my sister had felt when she and Danny had had their huge fight. "Terry, that blanket is 100 percent wool, so I have to take it to the cleaners. I keep telling myself I have to go there, and then I get busy and forget. Since it's been out so long, I don't see it any more, and besides, Chelsea Marie is using it for a bed now." He seemed to understand.

I told him I really didn't think that the messy house would be a problem between us, because it had been bothering me for a couple of months and I intended to change things. I explained, rather defensively, that our book *Side-*

tracked Home Executives was wonderful for organizing household cleaning chores. I pointed out that my house was immaculate as far as floors, windows, bathrooms, woodwork, and everything else was concerned. He agreed that was true, and he seemed to be relieved I was aware of the other problem. Grateful that the discussion was over, we let the flickering candlelight and music regain their hold on us.

Spurred by the stimulating dinner conversation the night before and impressed with my sister's successful cleanup campaign, I decided I'd try the infraction game on MY family. Since Peggy had told me that during the first week they played the game she hadn't really charged the money, I decided to do the same thing.

I went through the house with four infraction cards (one for each person) and about fifty bright red dots. Instead of tagging something, putting the time on the dot, waiting an hour, and then writing the infraction on the card, I decided to dot and infract at the same time. I figured that, since I wasn't going to charge money for the first week, there was no need to give anyone an hour to put his or her things away.

In fifteen minutes I had filled up all the cards and had to write on the back of Mike's and mine. I put a dot on everything I could see that should be put away.

I discovered during the dotting process that, like the Fourth of July blanket, many of my belongings hadn't seemed like clutter to me. I had become oblivious to the fact that they contributed to the overall messiness of the house. The rule in Peggy's home—"If it isn't decorative, it isn't out"—didn't seem to apply to me. I had to be very careful to be objective. Did my pocket calculator really look that pretty on the kitchen counter? Was the world globe that attractive in the bathroom? (That room had the best light in the house, and Joanna and I had taken the awkward ball in there to examine Indonesia with my magnifying glass.) Were my shoes an accent under the lamp table? Was my purse a nice touch, hanging on the dining room chair?

When I finished dotting everything, the house looked as if somebody weird lived there. At twenty-five cents each, the infractions added up to a total of $14.75 that we would have had to pay if this weren't a probationary week. I didn't put away any of my stuff, because I wanted the kids to know that this was a problem we all needed to work on, including me. I couldn't wait for each of them to get home from work so I could show them what I'd done.

When I get a new idea in my head, whether I think it up myself or get it from somebody else, I lose all sense of timing. Invariably, I prematurely jump into sharing before the sharee has had a chance to think. Like the time I came home from Weight Watchers and shared the water rule I had learned with my sister. Marilyn, the group leader, had told us that she had lost 120 pounds in fourteen months, and that in the few weeks she didn't have a weight loss, she could directly attribute it to NOT drinking eight glasses of water. Peggy said she and Danny would try to follow the rule. Later she told me that Danny had bucked at the idea because he said he'd feel like a fool, filling an eight-ounce glass at the drinking fountain in the police station.

I knew there had to be a solution. A couple of weeks later, as I was drinking one of my waters, I got the idea to count the gulps it took to finish the glass. It took fifteen gulps. I immediately called Peggy and passed on the information. She called Danny and he said he'd try out my idea. It wasn't until the next day that I found out he was mad at me. She said that he had had trouble the day before, drinking so much water. He had called her from work and complained that he couldn't leave the station for very long, because he had to keep going to the bathroom. Peggy had told him that I said that, when you first start drinking the amount of water you need, it will seem like too much because you aren't used to consuming the proper amount.

The next morning while he was standing at the sink, drinking his first glass of the day, Danny had inadvertently started counting his gulps. It seems it only took five swallows and the glass was empty! How was I to know that people's gulps are different? We figured that Danny must have drunk about forty glasses of water that day. It was no wonder he couldn't leave the police station.

This new game idea was far more exciting than gulping water, and I could hardly wait for the kids to get home. As usual, my enthusiasm for a new idea caused my timing to be terrible. Mike came home first. I nailed him just as soon as he was through the door. I didn't give him a chance to unwind and cool off from the summer heat; I slapped the infraction card in his face like a ticket-happy cop and started in on him. "Mike, things are going to change around here, and I'm starting with you. This is what you call an infraction card. It's got your name on the top, and your sisters and I each have one of our own. I went around the house today and I found twenty-seven clutter violations on you alone! That comes to six dollars and seventy-five cents!"

"What? Why?"

"Each infraction costs twenty-five cents, but I'm not going to charge you anything yet. You'll have a week of probation. But just look at this." I handed him the official-looking infraction card. "There are dish, glass, spoon, and fork infractions, some dirty underwear violations, and some miscellaneous messes, like the shaving stuff you left out. That one mess alone would have cost you one dollar and twenty-five cents!"

"Mom, chill out!"

"Do what?"

"Chill."

"Don't get sassy with me, Michael. This is my house, and if you are going to stay here, you will have to live by the rules! From now on, nothing will be left out unless it's decorative. That means your briefcase and backpack are out of the living room. That also means if you eat a piece of pie and you don't clean up after yourself, it will cost you a dollar and a quarter. A quarter for the knife you used to cut the pie, a quarter for the plate, a quarter for the fork, a quarter for the glass of milk you drank to wash the pie down, and a quarter for the crumbs you left when you cut the pie.

"See, what you'll do is, when you cut a piece of pie, you'll put the knife in the dishwasher. Then when you pour yourself a glass of milk, you'll put the milk carton away. Then you'll eat the piece of pie, drink the milk, and put the dish, fork, and glass in the dishwasher with the knife. Then you'll brush the crumbs off the kitchen counter into your hand and throw the crumbs into the garbage can under the sink. No, on second thought, you'll clean up the crumbs BEFORE you eat the pie. Oh! And if the bag under the sink just happens to be full, you'll empty it in the garbage can in the garage." I was out of breath.

"Mom, is there pie?"

"No, that was just an example of a typical mess I end up cleaning up. I'm not going to do it any more. I'm sick and tired of being everyone's slave. Oh, I almost forgot. If you have friends over, you will be infracted for their messes. I can think of one particular night of entertainment that would have cost you about eleven thousand dollars!"

"Mom, it's a hundred two degrees outside. Could I get out of this suit before I clean up my stuff?"

"Yes, but after this week there will be a time written on an infraction dot. The rule at Aunt Peg's house is that you have an hour from the time you are dotted."

Peggy Ann came home next. She had been working at Super Tan as a receptionist.

"Peggy, this is called an infraction card. On it is a list of items you've left out. It adds up to five dollars and fifty cents."

"Mom, I'm sunburned, and you know I don't have five dollars and fifty cents. Besides, you didn't give me any warning!"

"I won't start charging for a week."

"How am I supposed to pay after a week is up? I have to save my money for college!"

"Well, maybe you'll have to quit school."

I explained the rules in detail to her, and I had one more kid to go. Like a spider, I waited for Joanna to get home from her babysitting job. She was the least guilty of messes. She came in around 5:30 and plopped down on the couch with a growl. "Oh, those Hinds kids! What a couple of brats! Mom, you wouldn't believe how awful they are! The parents don't believe in saying 'No!' Jamie got mad at me because she wanted to watch cartoons and I was watching 'Days,' so she went over and pulled the cat's tail. Sometimes when she gets mad at me, she takes it out on the cat. So I go, 'Don't be mean to the cat!' and she goes, 'She likes it,' and I go, 'I'm sure! She does not.' Then Mark comes in and he flicks the TV while we're arguing. Oh, Mom, I don't know how I'm going to last the whole summer over there."

"Joanna, I'm sorry, but I have to change the subject for a sec. This is an infraction card. Notice your name is on it. So far today, you owe one dollar and fifty cents. You left out your manicure stuff, and you need to take the blanket that's in the hall and put it out in the car. I'm going to take it to the cleaners."

"Mom, that's not fair. Mike and Peg have junk out all over the house."

"I know that, and from now on it's going to cost them." When I explained how the new system worked, I could see the money light go on in her little blonde head. Her natural ability to keep things neat would now pay off in cash.

The system soon worked wonders in our house, and if it hadn't been for the fact that I jumped on my kids before they had a chance to relax after work, it would have been an almost perfect transition. It was not surprising that in that first week of playing the game, I was the one with the most infractions. Mike was a close second, Peggy Ann was third, and, of course, Joanna would have won the pot.

I have to say there were quite a few fights at the refrigerator, where the infraction cards were taped. When you are guilty, it's very hard to find out that you have been written up for something, but it makes you nuts to be written up when you are innocent. A good example was the time Mike wrote Peggy up for leaving a cereal bowl in the sink. Peggy was innocent, so she crossed through the infraction notation with a bold line and wrote, "NO WAY!" Then she turned her vengeful pen onto Joanna's infraction card and wrote her up for the bowl. By the end of the day, the children's cards were severely defaced by the dueling pens, and the cereal bowl was mine.

We had to make a rule that NO ONE was allowed to cross off an infraction without a group hearing. We decided to have a question mark infraction card so that, if there is doubt about an item, it can be written up and investigated later.

I discovered that, just as at Peggy's house, if the infraction cards were not posted every week, the house would fall back into a state of chaos. It was maddening to think that a few stupid little 3 × 5 cards and some fluorescent red dots stood between clutter and order, but it was wonderful to realize that those simple tools worked to change things drastically.

One morning, while we were talking to our agent, John Boswell, discussing the proposal for this book, he asked, "Why do you really think the game works so well?" We both said it was the money that spawned such enthusiasm. He laughed. "Do you mean to tell me that you think a forty-year-old man is inspired by a pot of change at the end of a week?" We had to admit that that did sound a little stupid.

"You guys really don't know, do you?"

"Well, then, smartypants, why DOES it work?"

"Competition. It's plain and simple ... COMPETITION!"

We had to think about that for a while. It was true that competition was half of it, but we realized that there was more ... the other half was GOOD SPORTSMANSHIP!

From the time men are little boys (and we know this from rearing three of them ourselves), they are taught to be good sports, and they will do nearly anything to prove that they are. Competition is inherent in the genes of every American male. It's the sport of it, and in any competition "good sports" play by the rules.

Ice hockey is a perfect example. We went to a game once and thought it was hysterical that tough, aggressive athletes would be willing to sit in a naughty box for breaking a rule by being too wild. There isn't a man alive, in his right mind, who would consent to sit somewhere in a pen as a punishment for being unruly, unless it was one of the rules of the game.

Call it good sportsmanship and you can get eleven tough men to stop frantically grappling for an elusive football ... just by throwing a hanky into the air. Call it good sportsmanship and nine giant men will stand with their toes exactly on the line, while the player who was roughed up gets one or two chances to throw a ball through a ring without anybody messing with him.

Call it a game and a man will pay thousands of dollars to be part of an elite club, wear special clothes, and drive a popsicle-type truck all over several hundred acres of grassland, smacking a little dimpled ball toward designated holes in the lawn. In the name of good sportsmanship, the same man who leaves his dirty tracks across a newly waxed kitchen floor will actually stop his game and rake his footprints out of a patch of sand he's had to walk through to whack his ball out of the grains.

Sportsmanship at home! That was it! It was competition and being a good sport that motivated each person in the family, especially the man of the house, to play by "the new house rules of order." We think that, on the playing fields, competition motivates athletes to win, because they hate to lose. We also think that the rules for good sportsmanship were invented because the athletes wouldn't play fair without them. If we were right, our home Infraction game would work with anyone who loves that "Wide World of Sports."

We all know that women are not going to get the cooperation they need from men by using the old feminine tricks of whining, manipulating, conniving, and nagging. Butting egos with the opposite sex doesn't work, either. It's time to try a fresh approach, one that includes LOVE and LAUGHTER. One with a united motive: more time to spend with each other, loving, laughing, and living in a home where there is peace, joy, and order.

Thirteen

The 50/50 Family

Once your husband realizes how important HE is to the success of a messless house, you are on your way to a 50/50 family.

Our definition of a 50/50 family is one in which the husband and wife stand together as an example of cooperation. To be that wonderful example to the children, the mother and father, if they both work outside of the home, must spend an equal share of time and energy on household maintenance and childcare. That doesn't mean that one week the husband cleans the toilet and takes the kids to ballet lessons, and the next week the wife does it. It means that the couple is more aware of the time and energy each spends working at home, and there is a sincere attempt to share the enormous burden, equally.

Today about 50 percent of all marriages end in divorce. Statistics show that it is usually the woman who throws in the towel, along with all the rest of the laundry. Judging by most of the people we know who have divorced, we think that almost all of those marriages probably could have been saved. Perhaps the truth behind courtroom scenes is that the couples aren't as overwrought with each other as they are with their SITUATIONS. When a situation gets out of hand, it's easy to lose your perspective and confuse the two. If the house is a mess and all you do is complain and whine, pretty soon no one listens to you. Everyone knows how long you'll nag before you explode, and they'll ride your fuse to the wire. If you choose to keep quiet and pick up after everyone yourself, you end up feeling like a martyr. Your resentment escalates, and before you know it you are a gritchy, exhausted lump of nagging humanity. You feel as if nobody cares. You look at your husband and children in anger instead of understanding. You feel a sense of futility.

The good news is that being upset with a situation is far less critical than being upset with a person, because you can change situations. Homes CAN become neat and stay that way. When a house is orderly and the woman is no longer solely responsible for making it that way, she will then have more energy to be fun-loving, kind, and nurturing.

With everyone working together, housework is not the giant bore it used to be. Even the kids do their share of the action cards. Through the years, as we improved our system, we came up with a great way to compensate them.

Each action card has a time estimate on it. That number is the key to our point system. We assigned a point value to every job in our homes, according to how long the job takes. We made each point equivalent to one minute of help. For example, if one of the cards says it takes twenty minutes, that job is worth 20 points. We keep track of points on charts that are posted in a central place.

A chart (see an example of one of our charts on page 195) has a place for the person's name and columns for the description of the job; the point value (20 points for twenty minutes); parent verification (each job must be inspected by a parent and initialed); the date; and the balance forward. A running balance is kept so that at any time it is very clear how many points a person has. The points are worth money, merchandise, or special parental services.

No matter what the age of a child, there are things he or she wants. Young children may want to have a friend spend the night or play at the park, go to the show or visit the zoo. Older children want the keys to the family car. Since children are always going to want SOMETHING as long as they live in your home, you have a perfect opportunity to teach them to help, in trade for what they want. This barter method impresses upon kids that life isn't free. There is a price for everything.

A value must be previously assigned to all of your services so that when one is needed your child knows how many points he or she must collect to afford that service. We post a list of services and their price. We charge 250 points for one of our children's friends to spend the night. (That service includes popping popcorn, renting a movie, and fixing a midnight snack.) To go roller-skating is 175 points. Charging points for using the car was inspired by Hertz—and the teen is charged by the mile. You need to set your own value on services, based on how valuable they are to your children, and it is very important to have it in writing!

If the points are cashed in for money, we decided that one cent per minute was sufficient payment for simple jobs. Sweeping the deck would be worth twenty cents if the sweeper wanted to convert his or her work to cash. Bigger jobs for bigger kids, such as washing the car, fixing dinner, mowing the lawn, or cleaning the fireplace, would have a greater value than a penny a minute. You decide.

We have thought of several other ways children can rack up points. We give them for grades (As are worth 500 points, Bs are worth 300 points, and Cs just mean that the child has the privilege of living in the home through the next semester). We also give bonus points for compliments our children get from adults. For instance, if someone says one of our children was kind and gracious on the telephone, that compliment is worth 25 points. If we ever catch one of our kids being nice to his or her sibling, we give bonus points.

Any jobs that are performed voluntarily are worth double-point value.

If you are like we are, you hate the idea of keeping track of information, but once you post these charts (and you stand strong against requests without earned points), your children will begin to see the value in keeping track of the information on their own.

This chart idea has several uses. We have a friend who decided to use it to track the behavior of the guy she had been going with for three years. She loved him, but the man was a workaholic, and the relationship seemed to be stuck in the waist-deep piles of his work load.

She decided to keep a running balance of what he contributed to the relationship, the same way we keep track of our kids' job contributions. In time it was clear that the beau wasn't committed to the relationship with the same quality of caring that our friend was. After charting him for several months on paper, she could see, in black and white, that the man spent very little time and energy enriching their relationship.

He received 250 points for remembering her birthday and another 100 points for giving her a card with a puppy on the cover, since she loved dogs. She gave him several hundred points for just being great company (the one day a week they saw each other). He lost 200 points when Valentine's Day came and he gave her a scraggly potted geranium with the PayLess sticker still on the bottom of the plastic flower pot. (This man was not cheap. He had just run out of time and opted for a quick stop at any open store he could find.) He gained 350 points for fixing her dripping sink and 400 points whenever he said "I love you," rather than "Me, too." Because she was usually the one to say it first, the courter only picked up 800 points.

He lost 2,000 points for not being with her when her dad had open-heart surgery and 500 points for not calling to see how he was doing. He got docked another 1,500 points for letting her think he had gone to Germany for three weeks when, in fact, he had stayed home and caught up on back work that all workaholics always have. He lost points every time he waited until Friday to call for their one weekend date. Every time he was late, it cost him 100 points (which totaled 1,200 points over the three-month period she charted him). The chart went on and on, and in the end, even though she loved him, she broke up with him.

Life has a way of slipping away, and if it is not going in the direction you want it to, you could end up wasting your life in the hopes that someday things will change. Charting what is happening will put your life in a different perspective.

Pam ... er ... our friend didn't show the man his point chart, because she fell in love with Terry and ceased caring if the man changed or not. The gray flannel suitor went away without the slightest clue that he was 3,550 points in the hole. Perhaps if he had seen his behavior in writing, he would have had a desire to change, but as far as our friend knows, he is probably repeating the same neglectful behavior in his current relationship.

We think one of the reasons that sports are big all over the world is because of the word "point." If points were not bestowed in games, no one would care much about the activity taking place on the field or court or table or any other surface. If you think about it, points are really silly. Yet everybody keeps score. We ask the score, argue the score, boast the score, celebrate the score; and the only way to have a score is to keep track of points. What is a point, anyway? A point is a unit of value in the eye of the beholder.

We learned early in our business career, working together almost every day, that points were valuable to the two of us. We are always giving each other points for remembering things, for knowing something the other one doesn't know, for working longer than the other one. We never keep track of them on paper, and we wouldn't know what to do with them if we did, but they have given us a real, tangible energy that mysteriously accompanies appreciation.

It is not easy for some people to give and receive compliments. Maybe they don't know what to say or how to say it. It is also socially unacceptable to ask for compliments, even though most of us would love more recognition. For us, the points have turned into a wonderful way to recognize each other's value. Whenever either of us feels we have not received enough credit for something we have done, it is so much easier to say, "Hey, I need some more points for that" than to say, "I need to be told how great I am for doing what I did."

We suggest that you take the chart on page 195 and make several copies. Give one to each of your children and explain how the reward system works. If you are going to start infracting the people in your house, you might as well get them all started helping more with the housework at the same time.

Previously, we instructed workshoppers, "Establish order yourself first, and your family will follow your lead." That's a crock! Well, it's partly a crock. It is true that if you want to have things change in your house, it will help if you change some of YOUR messy habits before you start involving your family. (Chances are good that you are one of the major contributors to the havoc in your home.)

We suggest that you spend at least a week watching yourself. Before you get a bunch of colored dots and start slapping them on everything that isn't decorative, start mentally infracting yourself, and you'll end up becoming very aware of some of your careless habits. You might as well get a jump on your family. In that week, think about the changes that are going to take place in your home, and watch your husband and children to observe their infractibility.

With a week of self-observation on your side, you'll be ready to present this new plan to your family. But one word of caution. Positioning is crucial, and just as our government spends years positioning itself for Mideast peace talks, you need to be very careful about the timing for yours. Your FIRST shot is going to be your BEST shot! Prepare for it. Have it in writing when you talk to your husband. Then the two of you can present it to the children as a united front.

We know that a 50/50 deal is a little unreasonable to expect, at least at first; but the trend is far more important than instant results. (A potato baked in the oven at 400 degrees for an hour is so much better than a russet nuked for ten minutes in the microwave.)

People really do not like change, especially if it means more work. Be patient and praise every bit of improvement you see in your family. There is nothing more effective than appreciation in speeding up the trend of cooperation.

The change that will take place in you will be especially wonderful. The time and energy you used to spend trying to get cooperation will now be there for you to use for more positive things. Your family will be amazed at what a different person you are. You won't be nagging anymore. You'll have leisure time to nap, play, and relax, and you will be so surprised that at the end of the day you will actually have energy left over for romance.

Family values are in a transitional time right now. The new direction must be toward more cooperation. If each member of your family can clearly see that the changes will benefit everyone, then a 50/50 family is definitely a possibility in your home.

POINT CHART FOR:

DATE	ACTIVITY	VALUE	BALANCE FORWARD	✔

Fourteen

A Mother's Day That Really Was

From Peggy:
  A few days before Mother's Day last year, Danny said to me, "This year we're going to do something different for Mother's Day! We're not all gonna go out for dinner and stand in those long lines, waiting for a table, like we do every year." I stared at him suspiciously. Surely he wouldn't DARE suggest that I prepare the meal! So what did he have in mind? "I'm going to take care of the dinner myself," he boasted. My suspicion turned to concern.

Danny is not renowned as a chef. Over the last few years he had learned a few basics, but a galloping gourmet he was not! True, he'd made great strides since that first Saturday breakfast he'd fixed and brought to me on a tray. I had been given hot coffee and a bowl of chili with onions and cheese sprinkled on top. (My niece, Joanna, was spending the weekend with us and later she told her mom, "There's no place like Aunt Peg's on a Sunday, but you never want to be there on Saturday!")

Being careful not to show my true feelings, which I feared would discourage Danny's efforts, I was falsely delighted with the breakfast. "Mmmm ... chili ... with onions, too ... I'll bet this'll hit the spot!"

"Yeah, I couldn't control the onion very well, though, so some of the chunks might be a little too big. How do you keep it from rolling around while you're chopping at it?"

Now, just a short time later, he was a chop-o-matician. He'd learned the correct way to chop onions, slice mushrooms, cut potatoes, dice tomatoes, and cube cheese; but prepare a whole dinner for company?

"Really? You're going to do the whole thing yourself?"

"No, I don't think I'll do it all myself. I'll make it a potluck. I'll call my dad and your dad and Terry and get them to bring filler, but I'll do the main dish."

"Filler?"

"Yeah, you know, baked beans and stuff."

"Mmmm ... baked beans and stuff ... I'll bet that'll hit the spot!"

"I'll call everybody and set it up. Just give me the phone numbers and you won't have to lift a finger." Danny called the greenhorn trio, and each one agreed to bring the assigned "filler." Meanwhile, I made three follow-up calls to the mothers. I asked them to refrain from taking over, even if the food contribution was an embarrassment. The women agreed to sit back and let the men culinate.

Terry was the baked-bean man, but he hit a snag at the grocery store, trying to pick out dry beans that were the "right color." He called Pam for help. "The brown ones say 'kidney beans,' but aren't those what you get at a salad bar?" My sister advised him to go to the canned goods section (he knew the aisle number from his premarital days) and pick up a couple of B&Ms and then "doctor" them with just the right blend of sautéed onions, crumbled bacon, Worchestershire, Grey Poupon, garlic, and chili powder. He seemed semirelieved.

Dad was in charge of providing the salad, and as a

pleasant twist he chose a recipe called "Tropical Fruit Festival," the makings of which cost about thirty-five dollars. He elected to peel, pit, and prepare the fruit the night before (a decision that made Mom get out the Mylanta). Reading from the red-checkered cookbook, Dad was at an impasse. "Mom, where do we keep the bias?" "What?" "The bias, where is it? I'm supposed to cut this kiwi on the bias."

Danny's dad was assigned the dessert. He "U-picked" and finely sliced an entire flat of strawberries, purchased those packaged, yellow Styrofoamlike shortcake replicas, and a spray can of whipped aircream, and he was ready for the party!

The Mother's Day celebration was to commence at 2:00 P.M. on Sunday. At noon, Danny (the "entree"preneur) was still chaised out in his robe with the morning paper. As the stove's digital advanced, I couldn't stand it any longer! I didn't smell anything cooking, the table hadn't been set, hors d'oeuvres were nonexistent, and I broke.

"So, Babe, what're you going to serve for the main dish?"

"I don't know ... I thought I'd go to the Food Pavilion and see what looks good."

"Mmmm ... that should work."

"Yeah. Maybe I'll do a chicken."

"Uh-huh. Chicken's always good."

"Yeah. Do you have a recipe for that Veal Pavarotti stuff you make?"

"Veal Scallopini?"

"Yeah."

"Gee, Babe, do you really want to get that involved? It's past noon."

"Nah, I better not chance it. I guess I'll barbecue."

"Uh-huh. Good idea. You might want to be gettin' over to that Food Pavilion pretty soon now. I think you're gonna be losin' your light here before too long."

"Yeah, I'd better get my shower and head out."

I was a nervous wreck! Danny seemed oblivious to the fact that, in less than two hours, fourteen people would be sitting down at a blank table.

Returning from the store with an assortment of poultry parts, he went to work. He carefully scrubbed each one, as if preparing it for surgery. He made barbecue "dip." He said that he didn't want sauce; he wanted to dip the parts in the goop, not mess around having to paint them with a brush. I explained that the recipe would be the same, whether he dipped or painted. He was pleased.

He took the raw chicken outside to the cold Weber as if he expected to turn a knob, like on the stove, and the coals would be glowing. He brought the chicken back into the house and asked me where I kept the charcoal lighter fluid. The next time I looked outside, flames were high above the grill, threatening to torch the bill of Danny's baseball cap, and Danny was standing back, with new respect for the container of Squeeze-A-Flame. I had to look away.

It was two o'clock. With singed eyebrows and red cheeks, Danny greeted the hungry guests. The proud culinarians carried their efforts to the kitchen, like 4-H-ers bringing their entries to the fair. Each one eyed the other's exhibit, anxious for the judging to begin, but I reminded them that we couldn't eat until the table was set. They all looked disappointed.

I turned to the other mothers and asked them if they would like to join me in a game of pool while the men set their table. Although pool is nothing any of us would ever want to play, they all accepted the invitation.

Downstairs at the pool table, we realized that no one knew the rules, so we made them up. We called the game "Ball in the Pants," and it went something like this: We would all use the same pole and take turns hitting whichever ball looked good. If the ball went into one of the pockets, the hitter had to take it out and put it in one of her own pockets. If her pockets were full, she could put the ball any place in her clothing as long as it would stay there without dropping. (Mom was actually so good at it that she got to put two balls in her bra because her pockets were already full.) We were having a great time when Danny announced over the intercom, "Come on, everybody, dinner's on the table!"

"Okay," my sister lilted, "we'll be up as soon as the game is over." I covered my mouth to keep the gasp from transmitting into the kitchen, and we all got hysterical at the thought of turning the tables on our mates.

The table was set! The guests of honor had special plates, covered with shiny aluminum foil. (I learned later that the purpose of the foil was more functional than decorative. It was to save the men from having to wash the dishes!) We each took our places at the feast table. Everything looked delicious! We were quite amazed. In their preparations, the men had only neglected one small thing ... the children.

"Looks real good, Dad. Where are we supposed to eat?" Chris looked around for more plates. Danny grabbed a stack of paper plates for the six starving outcasts and let them serve themselves from our table. Reaching over the seated guests to fill their wobbly plates, they seemed like partakers of a hot meal at a soup kitchen. They took their pitiful portions and went off somewhere to eat by themselves.

The meal was delicious! The proud men traded recipes and watched to see whose dish was the most popular. When we were finished eating, I said, "Great dinner, Babe! How 'bout another game of Ball in the Pants, ladies?"

We left the men to their kitchen cleanup and retired to the family room. We found it interesting how fast they were able to finish their work. They didn't chat or nibble on leftovers; THEY CLEANED. They were janitorial teammates, there to do a nasty job and do it fast!

There was only one casualty that wonderful Mother's Day ... my ceramic turkey platter. (Danny had put the barbecued chicken on it and put it in a 400-degree oven to stay warm while he set the table.) We don't know how the men will outdo themselves next year, but we're going to let them try!

Fifteen

A Critical Message

From Peggy:

As you already know, we totally understand the problems connected with being disorganized. Mail comes from sister slobs who scrawl page after page on odd tablet paper they borrowed from their kids or motel stationery they brought home from a vacation. The envelopes seldom match, and often the paper and envelope are marked with a coffee cup ring, crayon, or some unidentifiable stains, which the writer apologizes for, explaining that if she rewrites the letter it'll never get mailed. The dates on the letters are usually several weeks earlier than the postmarks, indicating that lack of stamps probably held up the mailings.

Our pen pals aren't interested in the seven (or even three and a half) habits of highly effective people. We've already established that those books are for people who already are effective. Our readers aren't in the Superwoman syndrome; they're on a merry-go-round. One woman begged, "Please write a book on how to just get by!" We wrote back to her and gave her seven secrets of minimally effective people. Hints like: "Sleep in your jogging suit. It's better than hanging around the house all day in your nightgown. If you have to run to the store, spritz your hair with a bit of water, slip a sweat band around your forehead, smooth a little Vaseline on your face, over some blush, for an exercised look, and step lively down the aisles as if you're still in cool-down. If you've slept in the suit more than one night, you'll look just like a marathoner."

To the woman who had a critical, condescending husband who wondered what she did all day (besides raise three children under the age of four), we wrote, "Just before Mr. Tudball gets home from work, dab a bit of Pinesol behind your ears and around the doorjamb, get out the ironing board (put the dog out so he won't bark at the two-legged intruder), hang a bunch of clean shirts on several doors, and scratch your fingers across a chocolate candy bar so it goes underneath your fingernails. Meet him at the door with a kiss, show him your nails, and say, 'Are these working hands or what?' "

People who are born organized do not understand us. They would never think to tell somebody to fake organization. Ordell wouldn't dream of using our recipe for "the smell of apple pie."

Purchase an apple pie from your favorite bakery. Remove the pie from its cardboard box. (Burn the box or discard it in the neighbor's garbage can.) Place the pie in your own pie tin. Note: Bakery pies are usually eight inches, while most household pie tins are nine. If the store-bought pie is smaller than your tin, simply press the pastry down until it fits, giving it an even more "genuine" home look. Meanwhile, combine the following:

one tablespoon flour
one tablespoon cooking oil
one tablespoon water

one teaspoon each: cloves, nutmeg, and cinnamon
one apple core

Mix ingredients in a disposable tin (chicken pot pie size). Shove the apple core into the center of the dough and bake at 225 degrees, all day. (For the smell of pumpkin pie on Thanksgiving, substitute a chunk of the jack-o-lantern on the front porch from Halloween.)

Once in a while we get a letter from an "Ordelly" who is irritated by our orderly accomplishments. One woman typed a quick note to us on lovely bond with a matching envelope and wax seal. She said, "I just completed reading your book and found it very interesting. Little did I know, my natural knack for organization could bring me dollars. I regret not having been as clever as you, as I too could have marketed my skills."

Over the years, we have been intimidated by born-organized people. We are always defending ourselves against their condescending observations and remarks.

Ring, ring, ring ...

"Hello?"

"Ooooooooo, Sissy, that Lillian Buckflank makes me sooo mad!"

"Who?"

"She's so smug! I was at the Urgency Treatment Center today and she's a receptionist th ..."

"Sissy, what happened?"

"Nothing. Ally just needed her sports physical. But anyway ..."

"How come you didn't take her to Dr. Ruiz?"

"I found out you have to have an appointment way ahead, and I couldn't get her in before volleyball practice starts, so I had to take her to one of those walk-in places."

"Ooo. Where is it?"

"Over by The Sink & Shears."

"I've never been there."

"You know that place where they wash your hair and cut it and you go away wet, but it's real cheap and you don't need an appointment?"

"I know where you mean. I hate their commercial."

"They've got a commercial?"

"Just on channel 52."

"You watch channel 52?"

"Yeah, once in while I like to watch Dog Court, where the dog-control people catch dogs at large with no licenses. Then the owners have to claim 'em and tell how they got out."

"So how come you hate the commercial?"

"Huh?"

"The Sink & Shears commercial."

"I don't know. It just makes me mad."

"Oh, yeah, speaking of mad, back to Lillian Buckflank."

"I don't know her, do I?"

"She's Larry Buckflank's mom. You've probably never met her, but she's irked me ever since we were room mothers for Chris's kindergarten class. The first time we met, I was in that huge dog costume you made and I was late to the Halloween party because I'd run out of gas and had to walk all the way down Hazel Dell Avenue to the school. You know how heavy that dog head is!"

"How come you didn't take it off?"

"I was carrying three dozen melting Dixie Cups, and, anyway, at that point I thought it was better to keep it on as a disguise. I was embarrassed. I had to pass a street crew by the Grange and it was humiliating."

"Lots of grown-ups wear costumes on Halloween."

"Yeah, but it was Friday, and Halloween wasn't till Sunday. I was a hit once I got to the school, but Lillian, in her black skirt and white blouse, just stared at me and pointed out how late I was. The teacher had told us to wear costumes, but Buckflank's idea of a costume was to wear

Larry's Mickey Mouse ears with a red polka-dot bow pinned to 'em."

"Whoa, that's pretty creative."

"Yeah, really. Since we got organized, it's bugged her to death! Today she really rubbed it in about where I had to take Ally for her physical. She smirked, 'Why, Peggy, I thought you were supposed to be so organized.' "

"She's just jealous."

"But you know how it makes you mad when you get accused of being disorganized when it doesn't have anything to do with organization. We didn't know when practice was going to start, and when the school sent the letter home, it was too late to go to our family doctor. It was the school's fault. Then you show up as a desperate walk-in and YOU look like the one who didn't plan ahead."

"Yeah, and somebody like Buckflap ..."

"Flank."

"Whatever ... would just tell her kid, 'Volleyball's out!' She couldn't handle the curve."

"Yeah, that's probably true."

"I think that the truth is, Lillian would probably like to be more like you. I'll bet she doesn't have a playful bone in her body."

"Maybe you're right. Once when we were doing the hearing tests on all the kids, she said, 'Oh, Peggy, you'll appreciate this. I did something the other day that made me think, *That's something crazy like Peggy would do!*' "

"I hate it when people use words like 'crazy' instead of funny."

"Yeah, like you're nuts or something."

"So what'd she do?"

"I was hoping it would be something like the dog suit deal, but she said, 'The other day at the bank, I made my deposit like I usually do, and when I got home I realized I had forgotten to get my deposit receipt. Well, I went straight back to the bank and told the teller that I'd forgotten to get my receipt and she said she knew I'd be back! Well, we had our little joke, but when I got out to the car, I checked my receipt against my check stub and I realized that I had accidentally put my paycheck in checking instead of savings!! I laughed so hard I thought someone was going to hear me.'"

"HO, HO, HO, what a riot!"

"Yeah, I wish you could have seen my face, listening to her."

"I can picture it. It's the same face I've had listening to you tell the whole thing."

"You want to go over to Mom's?"

"Yeah, what time is it?"

"Five to four."

"FIVE TO FOUR? I was supposed to pick up Ally after practice at 3:30!"

The truth is, as Sarah Lee says, "Everybody doesn't like something." If you get accosted or get put down by some humorless ho ho when you know you are doing your best, don't forget who the accostee is. That person probably vacuums indoor pets and is so knotted up inside that personal validation can only be found in someone else's turmoil. You are the heartbeat of your home! You'll never be so rigid that you can't change directions. You'll never put things before people. You'll never give up having fun. Although it is the most demanding, complicated, and mind-boggling of life's commissions ... you are a HOME-MAKER!

FROM PAM:

If you have read any of our other books, you know that I had an extremely unhappy marriage, but today I am remarried and happy beyond anything I could imagine! My first husband was cantankerous, cranky, and critical, and I have tried to help other women who have chosen to live with a person bearing those difficult three "C"s.

We know, from reading our mail from people all over the country, that most of the homemakers who are getting their acts together have husbands and families who are supportive of their desire to get organized. The hundreds of success letters we receive yearly usually express appreciation for supportive spouses. It doesn't surprise us to hear of the great and wonderful changes that happen when loved ones nurture and sustain the one who is challenging a major problem like being disorganized. It also doesn't surprise us when we receive letters asking for help from those who do NOT receive encouragement and even receive criticism from the people closest to them.

When I was a slob, my husband and I fought daily over the mess. He was frustrated with me and rightfully so. After all, I was a full-time homemaker and he worked very hard in the business world. Today, I can put myself in his place and feel how powerless he was to get me to change something that affected both of us. I know people can change, but they do it when they are ready. There is a wise saying: "No one can make anyone do anything they don't want to do."

In my case, on June 16, 1977, when I really decided I wanted to change, we had three children, ages twelve, nine, and three. For fourteen years we had struggled with the effects of MY problem. However, when I began to get control of things, my husband did not support me. He subtly put me down with comments like, "I wonder how long this kick is gonna last?" or "I told you that's what you should do, years ago. Now you're acting like it's your big idea." He would shake his head and point out all the things that were still out of control, instead of acknowledging the changes that were gradually taking place.

We keep telling you that climbing out from under the rubble takes time. It's the trend that counts. No one gets into a mess overnight, and no one will get out of it in twelve hours.

In the beginning, the person desiring to change has a lot of self-doubt. Criticism only confirms that self-doubt and prolongs the time it takes to truly change. I know from experience that criticism took its toll on my energy level, back when I was getting organized. Energy I could have used to chip away at the problem. My sister and I are very thankful to have been raised by wonderful parents who taught us to allow no one to cause us to doubt our ability to succeed. I used that idea over and over again when faced with my husband's negativity, and I won the battle in spite of him.

If you are married to a critical person, you have two options. One, you can let him win and you both lose, because you'll eventually give up and quit. Or you can get stronger! (The person with a supportive husband doesn't have the benefit of that negativity.) It takes an extremely strong person to take flack from another individual and still win. When you win, so will the critical partner (at least, as far as your problem is concerned). Remember, people who are critical have a much bigger problem than people who are disorganized. A person who criticizes was usually criticized when he/she was a child and consequently has extremely low self-esteem, which usually messes up relationships, not rooms in houses.

You have your work cut out for you. If you are married to a critical husband, he has his work cut out for him. Do not let anyone, husband, sister, mother, mother-in-law, friend, ANYONE, cause you to doubt your ability to succeed! You will succeed if you want to, with or without the support of someone else; and when you have accomplished your goal, it will be of little consequence that someone in the background was less than a mature person about his/her part in the picture.

If you are married to someone like my first husband, this is my advice from experience: do not waste your time and energy defending yourself, but convert both those commodities into tangible progress on your road to organizational freedom. Refuse to indulge in any form of defense. Instead, let his criticism be a trigger for you to clean out a drawer, iron a skirt, fold clothes, etc. Just make sure you are busy heading toward your goal every time you feel the pressure of the critic. Depending on how critical your spouse is, you could be triggered into getting much more accomplished than the person with a supportive husband.

Post 3 × 5 cards in a few strategic places with these words on them: I WILL NOT ALLOW ANYONE TO CAUSE ME TO DOUBT MY ABILITY TO SUCCEED. Also, remember that the critical person can change, too ... if he or she wants to.

Recently, I sat with a man (I'll call him Mark) on a flight from Chicago to Portland, and now I have new insight for those of you who have a critical spouse. Mark had been married for nineteen years and was very much in love with his wife, whom I'll call Sally. When I told him that my sister and I help the organizationally impaired and that we think it's genetic, he listened with great interest.

He told me his home was always a mess and he had tried everything to get Sally to keep it nice. As I guessed the kind of person she was, because I assumed she had the same wonderful attributes that all of you do, he was amazed that I could accurately characterize her. He was even more astonished when I could describe the condition of their home and know some of the things he was doing to try to get her to get organized. I'm sure he thought I was clairvoyant.

It's a four-hour flight from Illinois to Oregon, and in the air I realized for the first time how helpless a husband can feel when his home is out of control and yet he knows his wife is such a wonderful person. As I listened, I saw in this man utter desperation on one hand and total appreciation for the kind of person his wife was, on the other.

Mark raved about what a wonderful mother Sally was, how she had such a great relationship with their fifteen-year-old daughter, how close she and their eleven-year-old son were, how much fun she was at parties, how she loved to decorate, how happy she was most of the time ... the raving went on and on and on. When I said that you can't buy a good mother, a great hostess, a flexible, creative, spontaneous, and happy person, but you can pay for housecleaning help, he totally agreed. Yet he felt so powerless to have his home be the peaceful, clutterless place he craved it to be.

Then Mark told me something that I promised I would share in this book. He said that Sally really did not care that the house was a mess, or that she had gained forty pounds, so he had more or less given up any hope. When I told him she really DID care, he argued with me. I argued back. "Oh, she cares all right, but for nineteen years she has heard both your subtle remarks and blatant fits, and she is not about to let you know how she really feels about this problem, especially when she thinks there is no solution. She has pride, and to admit that she needs help, especially to another adult of equal value, would be too hard for her to do." He stared at me in disbelief. I told him that when I was a slob, I was very defensive because when I would decide to clean up the place, it never lasted. I'd get discouraged and go one more step backward in self-esteem. If you have acted as if this problem we share is no big deal, let your pride down and confess to your mate how it is affecting you. Mark was grateful to hear that Sally really was concerned, and he was eager to support her in any way.

Of course, he wanted to get all of our books and the card file, but I told him he couldn't have them. I said that Sally or her sister or a close friend would have to be the one to discover us. I made him promise not to go home and tell her that he had sat next to an author who writes books on how to get organized. He looked like a little boy who had just had his new bicycle run over by a garbage truck. I felt sorry for him.

You have the information, regardless of how you got hold of it. Now, the rest is up to you. We have great expectations for you. We know you can get your act together. If we could, so can you.

God bless you and your family.